# THE TRANSFERENCE IN PSYCHOTHERAPY
## Clinical Management

# THE TRANSFERENCE
# IN PSYCHOTHERAPY·
## Clinical Management

Edited by
EVELYNE ALBRECHT
SCHWABER, M.D.

International Universities Press, Inc.
New York          New York

**Library of Congress Cataloging in Publication Data**

Main entry under title:

The transference in psychotherapy.

   Based on a symposium sponsored by the American
Psychoanalytic Association, Nov. 1981.
   Bibliography: p.
   Includes index.
   1. Transference (Psychology)—Congresses. I. Schwaber,
Evelyne Albrecht. II. American Psychoanalytic Association.
[DNLM: 1. Psychotherapy—congresses. 2. Transference
(Psychology)—congresses. WM 420 T7715 1981]
RC489.T73T73    1984    616.89′14    84-12958
ISBN 0-8236-6625-5

Grateful acknowledgment is made to the Hogarth Press, Ltd., London, and Basic Books, New York, for permission to reprint material from *The Standard Edition of the Complete Psychological Works of Sigmund Freud*.

Manufactured in the United States of America

To my father,
Henry Albrecht,
and
to the memory
of my mother,
Augusta Albrecht

# Contents

# Contributors

*Jacob A. Arlow, M.D.* Past President, American Psychoanalytic Association; former Editor-in-Chief, *Psychoanalytic Quarterly*.

*Eleanor Galenson, M.D.* Clinical Professor of Psychiatry, Mount Sinai School of Medicine; member, New York Psychoanalytic Institute.

*Merton M. Gill, M.D.* Professor of Psychiatry, University of Illinois Medical Center, Chicago; Supervising Analyst, Chicago Institute for Psychoanalysis.

*Robert Michels, M.D.* Barklie McKee Henry Professor and Chairman, Department of Psychiatry, The New York Hospital–Cornell Medical Center; Training and Supervising Analyst, Columbia University Center for Psychoanalytic Training and Research.

*Paul H. Ornstein, M.D.* Professor of Psychiatry, University of Cincinnati; Codirector, International Study Center for Psychoanalytic Self Psychology.

*Evelyne Albrecht Schwaber, M.D.* Training and Supervisory Analyst, Psychoanalytic Institute of New England, East.

*Arthur F. Valenstein, M.D.* Clinical Professor of Psychiatry Emeritus, Harvard Medical School; Training and Supervisory Analyst, Psychoanalytic Institute of New England, East.

# Preface

In November 1981 the American Psychoanalytic Association sponsored in New York City a two-day Workshop for Mental Health Professionals, on "The Transference in Psychotherapy: Clinical Management." The climate of intellectual excitement and scholarly inquiry that pervaded the meeting led the participants to feel that publication of the proceedings would, given the broad range of views represented, be an important and responsive venture. This volume reflects the effort to record those exchanges—both formal statements and the informal dialogue between speakers and audience—that took place at the plenary sessions. Although approximating the original content of the presentations and discussion, this is not a transcript of the meeting. Editorial revisions have been made in each of the papers. The discussion sections have undergone minor stylistic changes but otherwise reflect the entire exchange. The editor's concluding remarks and the final responses by each of the authors to the questions posed in the introduction represent, for the most part, contributions subsequent to the workshop.

It is the hope of the contributors that this volume will further stimulate the spirit of scholarly exploration expressed so enthusiastically at the meeting.

# THE TRANSFERENCE IN PSYCHOTHERAPY
## Clinical Management

# 1

# Introduction

EVELYNE ALBRECHT SCHWABER, M.D.

The transference, as is well known, lies at the heart of psychoanalysis and was one of Freud's most central and profoundly creative discoveries. It is a powerful concept, speaking to the essence of the unconscious—the past hidden within the present—and of continuity—the present on a continuum with the past. Expressing the uniqueness of each person's experience and perceptions of another, it focuses and defines the domain of psychoanalytic inquiry: psychic reality. As it highlights our awareness that what we experience in another is a representation of the meaning we give to it, that what we see and feel is a product of what we bring to it, it may be viewed as a forerunner of the scientific revolution of this century, the era of relativity.

Freud spoke originally of two different yet related meanings of the transference (*Übertragung*). In chapter seven of *The Interpretation of Dreams*, in the context of a discussion of the importance of day residues in the elucidation of dreams, he wrote: "An unconscious idea is as such quite incapable of entering the preconscious and . . . can only exercise any effect there by establishing a connection with an idea which already belongs to the preconscious, by transferring its intensity to it and by getting itself 'covered' by it" (1900, p. 562). In this passage, transference refers to the attachment or transfer of an unconscious idea to a preconscious one.

The concept of transference also became delineated in its more commonly used meaning, that deriving from Freud's experience of the analytic relationship. There, feelings, wishes, and attitudes originating in a past relationship are transferred onto a present-day person. The one meaning suggests a spatial image; the other, a temporal one. In both cases the transference is evoked by some external occurrence and serves to lift unconscious mental content to its preconscious representation.

As the understanding of transference has continued to evolve, certain tensions have arisen; differing points of view have been espoused in conceptualizing its meaning and the implications of this meaning for interpretation. I shall formulate a number of the questions which have been debated, and to which the contributors respond in Chapter 10, recognizing that as I pose certain polarities there are, to be sure, a range of intermediate positions.

1. Is transference a phenomenon to be understood entirely within the intrapsychic realm, or, since it is experienced within the context of a relationship, thus taking on an interpersonal meaning, does this leave some measure of ambiguity as to whether we are including in our purview a realm of experience outside the intrapsychic domain? (This question is perhaps reflected in the different meanings originally assigned by Freud.)

2. As corollary to question 1, is the transference a distortion, a product of the patient's emerging wishes and defenses projected onto the image of the therapist or analyst—a distortion requiring ultimate correction—or is this a judgment not to be made? Is it rather to be viewed and articulated as a perception formed by the intervention of the therapist (or analyst) as this interweaves with and influences, in turn, the inner experience of the patient? Does the past and how it is represented distort the present, or does the present recreate and create anew the shifting imagery of the past?

3. As further corollary, is the transference to be relinquished on the path to psychic maturity or is it to remain part of an ongoing process influencing the continuity of development throughout life? Is it primarily an aspect of neurosis, a mark of immaturity, or is it a part of all life experience, a component of its depth and meaningfulness? Loewald (1960), arguing the latter view, cites an 1897 letter to Fliess in which Freud, recounting his experiences with his younger brother and his nephew between the ages of one and two, stated, "My nephew and younger brother determined not only the neurotic side of all my friendships, but also their depth!" (p. 30).

4. Is the transference but a single facet of the totality of the patient's experience within the clinical situation, a facet to be differentiated from such aspects as the therapeutic alliance or the real relationship? If so, is the transference in some sense not real, and is there a reality that does not include transference?

5. How do we understand the varieties of transferences other than the oedipal—the preoedipal transference, the primal or basic transference, or the selfobject transference—in which the analyst or therapist may be experienced as not entirely separate from ego or self? Have these varieties the same conceptual meaning as transference to a differentiated object? (In the context of the widening scope of psychoanalysis, this question has stirred considerable debate.)

6. How do we integrate the findings of the infant researcher—data derived from direct observation—into our understanding of transference? As we know, transference (in Freud's clinical usage) was discovered and articulated in the analytic situation, from which a history of development was subsequently derived. What are the implications for the understanding of transference if this process proceeds in the reverse direction—if, from the observation of infants

and children, the attempt is made to infer intrapsychic meaning? Is it possible to bridge the leap of inference that must be made here? (Mahler's observations of separation-individuation and Galenson and Roiphe's observations of pre-oedipal sexual development are but two examples of developmental research that has affected our understanding of transference.)

7. How do the positions taken on these questions influence the interpretive process? What do we interpret? Some will argue that only interpretations bearing on the experiential immediacy of the transference are efficacious; others feel that interpretations relating to broader aspects of the patient's experience may be meaningful as well.

8. Finally, how do we translate our position on these issues from the psychoanalytic to the psychoanalytically oriented psychotherapy situation?

As an addendum to these introductory remarks, I shall include here a section of the postscript to the Dora case—Freud's eloquent and stirring account of his failure to recognize, and his belated discovery of, the fundamental role of the transference:

What are transferences? They are new editions or facsimiles of the impulses and phantasies which are aroused and made conscious during the progress of the analysis; but they have this peculiarity, which is characteristic for their species, that they replace some earlier person by the person of the physician. To put it another way: a whole series of psychological experiences are revived, not as belonging to the past, but as applying to the person of the physician at the present moment. Some of these transferences have a content which differs from that of their model in no respect whatever except for the substitution. These then—to keep to the same metaphor—are merely new impressions or reprints. Others are more ingeniously constructed; their content has been subjected to a moderating influence—to *sublimation*, as I call it—and they may even become conscious, by cleverly taking advantage of some real peculiarity in the physician's person or circumstances and attaching themselves to that. These, then, will no longer be new impressions, but revised editions.

If the theory of analytic technique is gone into, it becomes evident that transference is an inevitable necessity. Practical experience, at all events, shows conclusively that there is no means of avoiding it, and that this latest creation of the disease must be combated like all the earlier ones. This happens, however, to be by far the hardest part of the whole task. It is easy to learn how to interpret dreams, to extract from the patient's associations his unconscious thoughts and memories, and to practise similar explanatory arts: for these the patient himself will always provide the text. Transference is the one thing the presence of which has to be detected almost without assistance and with only the slightest clues to go upon, while at the same time the risk of making arbitrary inferences has to be avoided. Nevertheless, transference cannot be evaded, since use is made of it in setting up all the obstacles that make the material inaccessible to treatment, and since it is only after the transference has been resolved that a patient arrives at a sense of conviction of the validity of the connections which have been constructed during the analysis.

Some people may feel inclined to look upon it as a serious objection to a method which is in any case troublesome enough that it itself should multiply the labours of the physician by creating a new species of pathological mental products. They may even be tempted to infer from the existence of transferences that the patient will be injured by analytic treatment. Both these suppositions would be mistaken. The physician's labours are not multiplied by transference; it need make no difference to him whether he has to overcome any particular impulse of the patient's in connection with himself or with some one else. Nor does the treatment force upon the patient, in the shape of transference, any new task which he would not otherwise have performed. It is true that neuroses may be cured in institutions from which psycho-analytic treatment is excluded, that hysteria may be said to be cured not by the method but by the physician, and that there is usually a sort of blind dependence and a permanent bond between a patient and the physician who has removed his symptoms by hypnotic suggestion; but the scientific explanation of all these facts is to be found in the existence of 'transferences' such as are regularly directed by patients on to their physicians. Psycho-analytic treatment does not *create* transferences, it merely brings them to light, like so many other hidden psychical factors. The only difference is this—that spontaneously a patient will only call up affectionate and friendly transferences to help towards his recovery; if they cannot be called up, he feels the physician is 'antipathetic' to him, and breaks away from him as fast as possible and without having been influenced by him. In psycho-analysis, on the other hand, since the play of motives is different, all the patient's tendencies, including hostile ones, are aroused; they are then turned to account for the purposes of the analysis by being made conscious, and in this way the transference is constantly being destroyed. Transference, which seems ordained to be the greatest obstacle to psycho-analysis, becomes its most powerful ally, if its presence can be detected each time and explained to the patient.

I have been obliged to speak of transference, for it is only by means of this factor that I can elucidate the peculiarities of Dora's analysis. Its great merit, namely, the unusual clarity which makes it seem so suitable as a first introductory publication, is closely bound up with its great defect, which led to its being broken off prematurely. I did not succeed in mastering the transference in good time. Owing to the readiness with which Dora put one part of the pathogenic material at my disposal during the treatment, I neglected the precaution of looking out for the first signs of transference, which was being prepared in connection with another part of the same material—a part of which I was in ignorance. At the beginning it was clear that I was replacing her father in her imagination, which was not unlikely, in view of the difference between our ages. She was even constantly comparing me with him consciously, and kept anxiously trying to make sure whether I was being quite straightforward with her, for her father 'always preferred secrecy and roundabout ways'. But when the first dream came, in which she gave herself the warning that she had better leave my treatment just as she had formerly left Herr K.'s house, I ought to have listened to the warning myself. 'Now,' I ought to have said to her, 'it is from Herr K. that you have made a transference on to me. Have you noticed anything that leads you to suspect me of evil intentions similar (whether openly or in some sublimated form) to Herr K.'s? Or have you been struck by anything about me or got to know anything about me which has caught your fancy, as happened previously with Herr K.?' Her attention would then have been turned to some detail in our relations, or in my person or circumstances, behind which there lay concealed something analogous but immeasurably more important concerning Herr K. And when this transference had been cleared up, the analysis would have obtained access to new memories, dealing, probably, with actual events. But I was deaf to this first note of warning, thinking I had ample time before me, since no further stages of transference developed and the material for the analysis had not yet run dry. In this way the transference took me unawares, and, because of the unknown quantity in me which reminded Dora of Herr K., she took her revenge on me as she wanted to take her revenge on him, and deserted me as she believed herself to have been deceived and deserted by him [pp. 116–119].

This was written in 1905, some eighty years ago. In reflecting on the various viewpoints presented in what follows, we might consider this question: Do they, despite their significant differences, retain nonetheless a fundamental commonality with the ideas expressed here by Freud?

## REFERENCES

Freud, S. (1900), The Interpretation of Dreams. *Standard Edition*, 4–5. London: Hogarth Press, 1953.

———— (1905). Fragment of an analysis of a case of hysteria. *Standard Edition*, 7:7–122. London: Hogarth Press, 1953.

Loewald, H. W. (1960). On the therapeutic action of psycho-analysis. *Internat. J. Psycho-Anal.*, 41:16–33.

# Part I

# 2

# Transference: An Introduction to the Concept

## ROBERT MICHELS, M.D.

The concept of transference asserts a central theme of psychoanalysis, that the past influences the present. Indeed in a sense psychoanalysis itself can be defined as the discipline that takes this essential biological perspective and applies it to the realm of mental life. However, this theme in itself, the influence of the past on the present, is too broad to serve as a definition of transference, and the history of the concept has been of a series of attempts to specify how the term should be limited.

Before discussing this further it is important to emphasize that for psychoanalysis the past that influences the present is not the past past, the past that is over, but the present past, the past that although labeled and thought of as ''past'' is alive and persists as an active dynamic force within the present. The psychoanalyst has no interest in what is actually over but is interested only in the living mental structure that may have originated in past experience but that continues alive as an active force within the mind; the persisting unconscious mental processes that shape the patient's current life. Although these processes originated in the past, we recognize that like other mental structures they may evolve and be transformed by subsequent development and experience. The past in which we are interested is the present past, different in important ways from the past experience of the patient (and, as we well know, even this past experience is itself different from the events that would have been observed in studying the patient objectively at that historic point in the past).

Transference phenomena are universal in all human relationships, but they have special significance in psychoanalysis and in psychoanalytic treatments. In considering most situations in life we try to emphasize the determining power of contemporary external reality—in other words, to control, limit, and minimize the apparent effects of transference. In psychoanalysis we do the reverse; we try to control, limit, and minimize the determining effect of contemporary external reality so that the transferential determinants of the patient's thoughts and behavior will be clear and vivid, both to the patient and to the therapist. In most social interactions transferential themes that do emerge are treated with some embarrassment; they are ignored, disavowed, or if enacted are rarely discussed. In psychoanalysis we do the opposite. We are interested in transference themes, we encourage their verbal expression, we are fascinated by any hint of them and try to foster their development, while at the same time we try to limit and minimize their enactment. Transference phenomena are important in understanding the powerful unconscious motivating factors that are present in all human relationships, perhaps particularly so in relationships that are strongly charged emotionally and that, like patient-therapist relationships, re-create aspects of early parent-child relationships. Transference phenomena are essential in understanding both the motivating and the resistive factors in any type of treatment, psychological or not. However, in psychoanalytic treatment they have an additional significance, because the treatment itself revolves around an exploration of the transference; here an attempt is made to use and study the persistent unconscious dynamic forces that shape the patient's relationship with the therapist rather than merely to accept their impact, positive or negative, on the therapeutic process. The exploration of the expression of these themes in the transference relationship is the essence of psychoanalysis and psychoanalytic therapy.

Transference responses are shaped by contemporary external reality as well as by persisting unconscious determinants from the past. Therefore the transference in psychoanalysis evolves in part in response to the psychoanalytic process itself. It is the exploration of this aspect of the transference, the development and evolution of transference phenomena within the relationship between patient and therapist, rather than the exploration of the initial transferentially determined attitudes toward the therapist that is at the core of psychoanalytic treatment. The concept of "transference neurosis," considered essential by some and superfluous by others, refers to the integrated cohesive transference that develops in the course of psychoanalysis and that encompasses the core themes of the patient's psychopathology in the newly developed relationship between patient and analyst—a constellation that may in some cases provide a substitute for the patient's neurotic symptoms.

Any aspect of mental life may be involved in transference responses—wishes, fantasies, emotions, defenses, attitudes, patterns of relationship with others, etc. Further, transferences may stem from any of the various developmental epochs. Transferences may be positively or negatively toned. They may motivate the patient or may stimulate resistance. They may be erotic or aggressive. At times they may be traced back to specific early relationships; at other times they may be seen as embodying mixtures of characteristics from several different relationships. Transferences have been classified according to each of these characteristics, and for specific purposes each type of classification may be useful. However, it is important to recognize that these are simply classifications of life, and that what we are talking about has a common theme.

Patients with certain types of pathology or certain character structures appear to have characteristic patterns of transference and there has been interest in delineating the specific transference characteristics or constellations of specific groups of patients. Some psychoanalysts have gone so far as to argue that the only true classificatory system of psychopathology or of types of patients must be based on the classification of the transference patterns that emerge in the course of psychotherapy or psychoanalysis and that other classificatory systems can be only tentative.

The exploration and interpretation of the transference is central to all kinds of psychoanalytic treatment. Positive transference feelings are important in motivating patients to seek out and remain in psychoanalysis or psychotherapy. Some trace these positive feelings to early trusting relationships with loving helpful parents and see them as providing the essential substrate for all subsequent successful therapeutic relationships. They differentiate them from other transferences by using terms such as the "therapeutic" or "working" alliance, and even suggest that these responses, the matrix within which therapy is conducted, should not be subject to exploration or interpretation. The capacity for forming such an alliance may be seen as an essential prerequisite for successful therapy and an impairment in this capacity as a major obstacle in the treatment of many sicker patients. There are interesting controversies regarding principles of psychotherapeutic and psychoanalytic technique related to the concept of the therapeutic alliance. Should this fundamental positive relationship be explored and analyzed? Should the therapist actively foster its development? And are there tensions or conflicts between these approaches—exploration and analysis on the one hand, fostering the alliance on the other? Does one approach impair the other?

Patients often struggle against the experience and particularly the expression of transference feelings in the therapeutic relationship. An important theme in psychoanalytic treatment is the analysis of what can be called resistances to the transference. This is one of the characteristics of psychoanalysis that contributes to the special intensity of the transferences within psychoanalysis and the pattern of their evolution. One of the current external realities of a patient in psychoanalytic treatment is a therapist who is interpreting resistances to the experience of the transference and encouraging the patient to recognize its development. This external reality shapes the evolution of the transference, as all external realities in all relationships influence the transference phenomena that emerge.

Transference themes are themselves important sources of resistance in psychoanalysis as in all treatments. The interpretation of transference when it functions as a resistance is important in all types of psychodynamic psychotherapy. The failure to recognize or deal with transference resistance is one of the most common problems in conducting psychotherapy.

Although it is common to think of psychotherapy as exploring the links between past and present, these links are already established in the transference and it is through exploration of the transference that they become central to psychoanalysis and much exploratory psychotherapy. A common misunderstanding of psychoanalysis would emphasize the discussion of the historic past and its relation to contemporary external reality as a core theme. However, if such discussion is conducted in arenas other than the transference it rarely has the emotional power or conviction that accompanies the analysis of the transference. Some have argued that the only really effective interpretations are transference interpretations. The degree to which this is true, the extent to which transference interpretations are qualitatively exceptional, as opposed to merely frequently important, is a matter of contemporary controversy.

The most common notion of transference refers to the mental life of the patient. However, transference may be used to refer to relationships in which the therapist participates. The first and most vivid indication of transference phenomena may be in the therapist rather than in the patient; hence the study of the therapist's mental life and behavior is an important source of information about the patient's transference. The patient in effect expresses the transference by eliciting, provoking, or seducing responses in the therapist. The extent to which there are unique mental mechanisms involved in this type of phenomena, the extent to which they have central clinical significance, particularly in the treatment of more disturbed patients, and the close link of this idea and certain technical notions emanating from it to specific schools of psychoanalytic thought is another area currently being debated.

Exploration of the transference entails not only exploration of the patient's response, the unconscious themes that shape it, and their origins in the past, but also exploration of the current situation that has precipitated it. All transference responses are real responses to contemporary stimuli; they are all more or less appropriate. Some of the most important transference phenomena are thoroughly realistic and adaptive. That something is transferentially determined by unconscious mental factors does not mean that it is wrong, pathological, or maladaptive. All of life is transferentially determined by unconscious factors.

This view of transference makes clear that transference is a universal characteristic of relationships. Although an earlier emphasis in our thinking suggested that transference stood in contrast to reality, the present view would make clear that transference is an essential determinant of all psychic reality. Reality without transference, were it possible, would be less than human. A corollary is that exploration of the transference does not explore how reality is distorted, but rather how the patient's personal reality is structured by his past. The word transference is the Latin equivalent of the Greek term "metaphor," both meaning the same thing—carrying across. It is this view of transference that emphasizes its centrality in the personal structuring of our inner world.

# 3

# A Developmental Approach to Transference: Diagnostic and Treatment Considerations

## ARTHUR F. VALENSTEIN, M.D.

The phenomenon of transference came to Freud's attention through the story of "Anna O," Breuer's famous case of hysteria, whom he treated between 1880 and 1882 and who developed what must have been an erotized attachment to him, culminating in a pseudocyesis. It so alarmed Breuer that he abruptly terminated the "chimney sweeping" therapy.

Freud, however, was very impressed by Breuer's account, and when they wrote their *Studies on Hysteria* (1895) Freud made a first reference to the phenomenon of transference in the psychoanalytic sense. Even that early reenactment within the treatment situation was specified as "a frequent, and indeed in some analyses, a regular occurrence," with the patient "finding that she is transferring on to the figure of the physician the distressing ideas which arise from the content of the analysis." As Freud further put it, "Transference on to the physician takes place through a *false connection*. . . . The content of the wish had appeared first of all in the patient's consciousness without any memories of the surrounding circumstances which would have assigned it to a past time" (pp. 302–303).

As Nunberg (1951) so nicely phrased it a half century later,

> transference is like Janus, two-faced, with one face turned to the past, the other to the present. Through transference the patient lives the present in the past and the past in the present. . . . The fact that the patient loses the sense of time in the transference situation is not surprising, as it corresponds to the phenomenon that repressed unconscious events, events of the past, are experienced in the present as if no time had elapsed. Indeed, we know from Freud that the unconscious is timeless [p. 5].

Is that all there is to transference—the revival and reliving in the treatment situation, through the transference neurosis, of the conflicts of "infantile life" as these pivotally emerge out of an incomplete or faulty resolution of the Oedipus complex (age 3-5 +), as it then was called? For during that first half-century—with only few qualifications—psychoanalysis was considered predominantly a conflict psychology so far as treatment was concerned. Its theory of neurosogenesis was based on a concept of infantile neurosis, with repression of predominantly oedipal but also preoedipal conflicts, the outcome being symptom formation. The corresponding theory of cure was that if the paradigm infantile conflicts were reactivated and recapitulated in the transference neurosis, they might be brought to consciousness, made accessible to insight, and resolved. The neurotic symptoms would fade away, as they had been no more than compromise expressions of the now resolved conflicts. Psychic integration, thereby enhanced, would further effective functioning. The implication was that once infantile memories, fantasies, and conflicts became conscious, there would be an opportunity to compare reliving the *past* in the present with living the *present* in the present, and for action consonant with the reality principle.

The neuroses which were found to be accessible to analysis were called the "transference neuroses," more recently termed the "structural neuroses," based upon the formulation that unconscious conflict—attributable to typically sexual and/or aggressive strivings out of the id which are opposed by the superego, to the detriment and inhibition of the ego—has become intrapsychically structured after considerable ego development has taken place. Cognitive functioning should have reached a secondary process level by that time. Self and object discrimination of an increasingly sophisticated nature would prevail, with a developed capacity for object love and a readiness for the internalization and consolidation of superego values in identification with more or less idealized objects.

In contrast were the so-called "narcissistic neuroses," considered inaccessible to classical psychoanalysis because such patients had difficulty differentiating self from objects. The presumption was they had failed significantly in resolving the symbiotic tie to the mother during the first year of life. Unable to invest others with interest and affection in their own right, these patients were likely to perceive others as simply mirroring the self or self needs, and to make them the *transference* recipients of archaic ideational constructions and affects projected from the self. Nowadays such disturbances are placed under the rubric of "developmental neuroses," based upon the formulation that these patients suffer their disorders—inclusive of the psychoses, the borderline conditions, the narcissistic character disorders, certain psychosomatic illnesses, and particular impulse and addictive disturbances—as a result of external conflict and of developmental traumas or deficits occurring *very* early in life, originating usually during the preverbal phase, when primary process mental functioning holds sway. This is the time of the first-year mother-child symbiosis and dyad.

It continues on, though, in such instances, into the second and even the third year of life.

Clearly such conditions are preoedipal, antedating the triadic transference potentialities of the oedipal period. In keeping with the developmental phase in which these disorders have their origin, the transference replications are predominantly dyadic, centering on needs for nurture and security, with attendant misperceptions and misconstructions of self-object discrimination. In consequence, at least through the initial and middle phases of treatment, the more interactive and experiential therapeutic features of necessity assume a temporal hierarchical priority over cognitive aspects, over the articulate explanatory content of interpretive interventions.

To return briefly to some further historical considerations relevant to transference and psychotherapeutic technique, transference was originally understood to refer particularly to the "transference neuroses," to the recapitulation of impressions and experiences from postverbal life and the genetically structured conflicts originating in or regressively from the oedipal phase, the paradigmatic "infantile conflicts." To be sure, Freud (1895) very early on spoke also of the necessity for a fundamental positive transference as a sine qua non for psychoanalytic work; only a basic "confidence" (p. 265) in the "personal influence" (p. 283) of the physician motivates a patient to "defeat the psychical force of resistance" (p. 301) against "the disclosure of the most intimate and secret psychical events" (p. 265).

However, in this latter respect, a somewhat different concept of transference is implied (Valenstein, 1974), one referring to

the earliest biopsychological determinants around which transference phenomena later coalesce. There are those aspects of patient response which do not find their way into articulate expression; not just because they are blocked by the resistance of acting out of the transference, whether in an analytic situation as such or outside of it, but also because they may not be verbally available to the patient, as a matter of development. Quite possibly he brings to the consulting room certain fixations and disturbances from very early in his life, just as he brings oedipal problems out of the post-verbal period of development [p. 313].

The confidence transference, what Freud referred to as the generally positive transference which makes therapy possible, was specified by Greenacre (1954) as "the basic transference, . . . the primary transference, or some part of primitive social instinct." She attributed it largely to "the mother-infant quasi-union of the first months of life" that acts as "a veritable matrix" (p. 672). Loewald (Valenstein, 1974) broadened this concept, suggesting that "Transference . . . in its most basic meaning has reference to [the developmental Anlage of] the individual's love life, the source and crux of his psychic development, in both its object-libidinal and its narcissistic aspects" (p. 312).

To refer briefly to the clinical concept of the therapeutic (Zetzel, 1956) or working (Greenson, 1965) alliance: I have already pointed out that from the very beginning of psychoanalysis Freud emphasized that the viability of a therapy depends upon a fundamental confidence transference—what he (1937) later referred to as a shared "love of truth." Alliance implies mutuality, which is in turn ascribable to the continuity of basic trust and the potential for growth through identification—qualities which emerge out of the developmental matrix of the early mother-child relationship. The satisfactory resolution of a series of normative developmental "crises" is essential in this process—basic trust versus mistrust, and next, autonomy versus shame and doubt—as initial tasks for growth and development during this early period, according to Erikson's psychosocial scheme (1950) of an epigenetic (ego) developmental unfolding. Should these normative "crises" be unsatisfactorily resolved, not only is significant ego deficit with a deficient sense of self (a flawed "sense of personal identity") likely to follow in consequence, but reciprocally, disturbances in the perception and response to objects will probably crystallize—to which, in due course, the transference falls heir.

It is relevant that Elizabeth Zetzel (1956) introduced the concept "therapeutic alliance"—which in fact she attributed to Edward Bibring, who in 1937 described "an alliance between the analyst and the healthy part of the patient's ego"—shortly after the discussion of a paper Michael Balint gave in Boston (1956). Recalling this at a subsequent panel, on which I also reported, I wrote (Valenstein, 1974):

> In that discussion it was brought out that there might have been something lacking in the prevalent primary attitude of such a (basic fault) patient to the analyst; something in the fundament of his earliest ties with respect to his predilection for *mis*trusting rather than trusting—and that this defect in object orientation might have escaped the standard analytic method of articulate free association.
>
> Valenstein continued: "It cannot be denied that there is a fundamental something in the relationship which stands as a foundation to the more subtle and later evolved transference nature of the relationship. However, it is also germane to question whether *everything* is necessarily transference that happens emotionally between patient and analyst, or between any two human beings, for that matter. Although it is true that there are increments of the inchoate past in every relationship, bringing these elements within the usual clinical domain of transference so broadens the term that it begins to lose some of its psychoanalytic and technical specificity" [p. 313].

Ontogenetically, we might look to the development of

trust as fundamental to primal transference, which qualifies the capacity for therapeutic alliance, pro or con. I formulated it as follows: The unborn child

> depends upon the host mother for survival and for the psychobiological fulfillment of essential developmental needs. In this sense "prototrust" begins *in utero* and continues into the neonatal phase and thereafter. . . . What does this mean for what later becomes basic trust or primal transference? . . . [with patients whose] transference reactions are beyond the articulate and the classically analyzable. Such patients may be suffused by primitive affects, and their "untamed" instinctual surges and responses bespeak the biopsychological substrate [pp. 313–314].

Massive and peremptory transference reactions relatively inaccessible to interpretation have diagnostic and treatment significance. They suggest a major ego developmental disorder beyond neurosis which requires a more active interactional, interpersonalized therapy—usually a reconstructive (in the sense of reparative structure building) and possibly corrective transference experience at the here-and-now level. In contrast, the so-called structural neurosis, in which a transference neurosis *gradually* evolves according to the patient's predilections, leads to a quieter and less active treatment situation, one in which the patient is far more accessible to interpretations and insight.

What makes the borderline and narcissistic character neuroses so difficult to treat is that the capacity for alliance is limited because the transference is of a narcissistic order or it borders on or may cross over into the psychotic. In both instances the patient is limitedly capable, at best, of making that kind of intercommunicatively trustful and basically realistic alliance to the therapist which is a sine qua non for the achievement of the therapeutic split essential to insight therapy; for insight therapy depends upon reciprocity between the self as observer—with a sense of objectivity and judgment in alliance with the therapist as therapist—and the self in subjective reexperience of the past. With respect to the latter, it is as if the therapist takes on the characteristics of pivotally important figures out of the past but is experienced in the here and now.

Individuals with borderline or narcissistic character pathology tend to construe transference feelings and perceptions literally as their *only* reality, and feel quite justified in so doing. As treatment begins, they usually sense and believe, more or less with conviction, that they are actual protagonists or antagonists vis-à-vis the therapist. This position is likely to preempt the relative therapeutic neutrality and benignly equidistant stance of the therapist. It is noted, quite correctly, that the feelings stirred up in the therapist, often generalized as countertransference—which they may or may not be in the narrower sense of that term—are informative as to the transference position and behavior of the patient, lived out or acted out in repetition of the past. This may be positive and seductive, excessively so, or negative and provocative to the quick.

Sooner or later such patients can no longer tolerate the therapist's remaining relatively ambiguous and limitedly active. The whole tempo of interaction within the therapeutic situation necessarily increases and becomes very lively indeed at times, because such patients seem intent on repeating in behavior rather than in words—in living out the past, warped into the present, as the only reality they know. They inveigle the therapist into becoming emotionally involved in response to their acting out in the transference. They induce him, if possible, to respond in kind, reciprocally, so as to fulfill and validate the transference as utterly real—for example, positively and gratifyingly to the infantile dependent position, seductively if it is erotized, or angrily and punitively in response to provocative devaluation or aggression.

To fill this out clinically, let me describe something of the characteristics of the "complete" narcissist. Fortunately, not every narcissistic patient has all these characteristics—a state of affairs that would be quite unmanageable—but these features are for the most part shared in common. These patients are indeed egocentric, absorbed in themselves, not empathic to others, but only responsive, as it were, to emotional qualities which they perceive as coming from others—either wholly projected onto the others from themselves, unconsciously so, or better still, inveigled from the others, hence validating and reinforcing the projections. They appear grandiose, as if completely and gloriously sufficient unto themselves, or paradoxically abject in their feelings of emptiness and parasitic helplessness. Relationships are not seen or experienced as mutual but are essentially manipulative, omnipotently so—and it is strategically necessary to be the manipulator ("king of the hill," "top dog") rather than the manipulated. In this respect, they are shallow in their values, and their loyalties, if one may call them that, are governed by opportunism. Everything is given over to their need to control and to exact gratification and reassurance as to their self-image. Not all of them *appear* to be noncommunicative and nonrelating. In fact, some may be gifted and use a surface charm to bring the other into their orbit, there to be further won over, only then to be ignored (inconsistently perhaps) or even threatened with rejection. Their motto might be, "The world is (or should be, or had better be) my oyster and I shall not want." Their sense of entitlement, of being special, is exorbitant, and they may be corrupt in exploiting others, with little internalized guilt, though they may fear hatred from others and/or rejection in a talion sense.

You can imagine what this does to the transference and

how this feels as it is acted out in relation to the therapist. It would truly take more than a strong man or woman—perhaps the literal mirror that Freud never intended in his use of that metaphor—or a nondirective rock if counterfeelings of significant degree were not to arise from time to time. These counterfeelings are not necessarily countertransference in the narrower sense of the word. After all, it *is* a bit much to be made to feel, as has been pointed out so well, indiscriminately ignored, as if one were a piece of the woodwork or simply a distracting interferer, to be personally disregarded or to be evaded or avoided. Or to put it another way, it may be quite wearing to feel so baited—so played upon, manipulated and tricked—as such people are wont to do, often beneath a veneer of socially attractive and ingratiating, even winning ways.

The problem is that the feelings stirred up in the therapist may go beyond understandable frustration and reciprocal feelings of distress and pleasure, if, for example, one is ployed and played with by a manipulative, winning individual. Residual lack of confidence or anxiety in the therapist, stemming from unresolved conflict affecting self-esteem, or the expression of aggression (which ordinarily would be substantially sublimated into the therapeutic work) is likely to be brought forward in its less advantageous form—that is to say, in retaliative form. Falling in with the dubiously complimentary attribution of therapeutic omnipotence invites countertransference reactions of just this sort, for if the therapist is overtaken by therapeutic zeal, he or she can very readily become entangled in or confused by the tactics of these difficult patients. It is essential that one remain clear regarding the nature of the disturbance. Keeping in touch with the clinical situation diagnostically, and empathetically with its phenomenological and therapeutic actuality, the therapist is oriented technically and in a position to avail himself of that measure of personal insight and clarity which reinforces him in his work. It enhances those qualities of patience and therapeutic poise which are so necessary, even (and especially) when one becomes the transference object of the more difficult patient.

## References

Balint, M. (1956), The theory of psychoanalytic technique. Presented to the Boston Psychoanalytic Society and Institute, October 27.

Bibring, E. (1937), Therapeutic results of psychoanalysis. *Internat. J. Psycho-Anal.*, 18:170–189.

Breuer, J., & Freud, S. (1885), Studies on hysteria. *Standard Edition, 2.* London: Hogarth Press, 1956.

Erikson, E.H. (1950), *Childhood and Society.* New York: Norton, 1950.

Freud, S. (1937). Analysis terminable and interminable. *Standard Edition,* 23:216–253. London: Hogarth Press, 1964.

Greenacre, P. (1954), The role of transference: Practical considerations in relation to psychoanalytic therapy. *J. Amer. Psychoanal. Assn.*, 2:671–684

Greenson, R.R. (1965), The working alliance and working through. In: *Drives, Affects, Behavior,* Vol. 2, ed. M. Schur. New York: International Universities Press, pp. 277–314.

Loewald, H.W., panelist (1974), Panel on "Transference" reported by Valenstein, A.F. *Internat. J. Psycho-Anal.*, 55:312.

Nunberg, H. (1951), Transference and reality. *Internat. J. Psycho-Anal.*, 32:1–9.

Valenstein, A.F., Reporter (1974), Panel on 'Transference.' *Internat. J. Psycho-Anal.*, 55:311–321.

Zetzel, E.R. (1956), Current concepts of transference. *Internat. J. Psycho-Anal.*, 37:369–376.

# 4

# The Thwarted Need to Grow: Clinical-Theoretical Issues in the Selfobject Transferences

## PAUL H. ORNSTEIN, M.D.

There is undoubtedly a growing consensus among psychoanalysts today that the transference is *central* to the treatment process in the psychoanalytic psychotherapies. It is my contention that this view has emerged from the simple fact that for psychoanalysts and psychoanalytic psychotherapists the patient's self-experience has always been most directly accessible via the study and working through of the transference. Transference has thus been naturally placed into the very center of our clinical and theoretical considerations. As Dr. Schwaber has noted in her Introduction, ever since *The Interpretation of Dreams*, in which Freud (1900) first articulated the mental mechanism of transference as a fundamental working mode of the mind, and ever since his report on the analysis of Dora (Freud, 1905), in

Modified version of a paper first presented under the title "Transference in a New Key" at the Paul G. Myerson Symposium on Psychotherapy—the fifteenth annual Tufts Symposium—"Transference in Psychotherapy: Current Conceptualizations," April 25, 1980; and of another version presented as one of The Lydia Rapoport Lectures (1981) at The Smith College School for Social Work entitled: "The Impact of Self Psychology on the Conduct and Process of Psychoanalytic Psychotherapy."

which he first articulated the clinical significance, role, and function of the transference, our theories of psychopathology and our theories of treatment have revolved around discovering the nature of this transference, its idiosyncratic manifestations and the various ways in which we respond to them, work them through, disregard them, or use them for therapeutic purposes.

Transference arises *spontaneously* in any form of treatment—in fact it arises in any extratherapeutic, everyday close relationship as well—most particularly in friendships and marriages—and is therefore rightly considered ubiquitous. However, when it emerges in the psychoanalytic psychotherapies, transference acquires a special quality, role, and function through the therapeutic responses to it. These responses essentially consist of *acceptance, understanding*, and *explanation*, regardless of the treatment setting.

The setting does, of course, contribute to what will emerge in the transference, but the special quality of the transference will arise out of the fact that it is not deliberately provoked or fostered but is allowed to emerge within a neutral, nonjudgmental, accepting, and development-enhancing climate of *optimum frustration*. This optimum frustration, the key condition for structure building in infancy and childhood, as well as in the analytic treatment process, can occur reliably and predictably only in the analytic forms of therapeutic relationship. For a variety of reasons it cannot occur in the extratherapeutic relationships I have mentioned. Nowhere else does the patient have as complete a chance for the mobilization of his transferences as in a treatment setting, without transference demands similarly being placed upon him by the person with whom he is interacting—as, for instance, in friendship or marriage. It is this complete centering upon the patient and his transference experiences in the analytic treatment process, inviting the regressive remobilization of pathognomonic transferences or their derivatives, that provides the basis for the unique healing process offered by the psychoanalytic psychotherapies.

It is the central position of this qualitatively different transference experience, then, that unifies the various psychoanalytic treatment modalities—brief, focal psychotherapy, intensive psychoanalytic psychotherapy, and psychoanalysis—and places them on a continuum. The notion of the continuum simply means that regardless of the specific treatment setting we choose, we are guided in our interpretive interventions by the same theory of illness and the same theory of cure. Furthermore, the timing and framing of our interventions will depend solely upon our understanding of the nature of the transference and the process of working through, as this is codetermined by the setting and goals of treatment. To put this another way, each treatment setting will allow certain aspects and a certain degree of depth of the transference to emerge. In focal psychotherapy only a small segment and a limited degree of depth will be in evidence, while in intensive psychoanalytic psychotherapy a much larger and deeper segment will be available. Finally, in psychoanalysis the fuller pathognomonic transference will emerge to take center stage in the process of working through.

By emphasizing the idea of a continuum here I do not wish to minimize the differences that may arise in the various settings and their respective goals, but I will not focus on these, as they are irrelevant to my main points in these brief remarks. The similarities, I would argue, are of more fundamental significance.

Hitherto two trends, to which I can refer only in passing, could be discerned in the various attempts to grapple with the problem of transference. Some efforts clearly focused on the pathology in the transference, coupled with an approach that appeared excessively technique-oriented (in the sense of what to do or not to do in response to the various manifestations of the transferences: the distortions, the regressive erotic and hostile components, etc.). Other efforts appeared to focus on those elements of the transference which facilitate the more limited goals of a treatment process (sidestepping some of the pathology) and on the experiences of the patient in the therapeutic situation that are essentially growth-promoting through identification.

It is of considerable interest to us today that this potential for growth via identification was thought achievable by a certain overall responsiveness of the therapist (the fostering of the real relationship or the therapeutic alliance) and by refraining from interpretations that aim at achieving drive-related and reality-related insights. It was explicitly recognized that these drive- and reality-oriented interpretations were somehow not growth-facilitating and may even have actively interfered with growth. The validity of these observations was well documented, but the reasons for it were not satisfactorily explained. I mention this only because I want to indicate later how far and in what direction we have progressed in this crucial area.

While, as I noted earlier, there is a growing consensus as to the centrality of the transference in the psychoanalytic psychotherapies, there is also increasing divergence of opinion about what constitute the central and clinically significant elements of the transference and how to deal with them. My presentation will (1) briefly focus upon some empirical data of a selfobject transference and then (2) describe the transference reactivation of the thwarted need to grow, highlighting a shift in interpretive focus which enhances the therapeutic leverage of the psychoanalytic psychotherapies. Let me preface the exposition of these views by saying that significant progress in psychoanalysis has always occurred when, in the sequence of the inextricable linkage of method of observation, findings, theories, and treatment principles, some "anomaly" was detected (usually first in the treatment process and its results) which then led to a chain reaction of refinements in the method of observation, to new findings and theories, and to new treatment principles.

## SOME EMPIRICAL DATA OF A SELFOBJECT TRANSFERENCE

To underline the assertion that psychoanalysis is an empirical science and that it is the shift in our "mode of listening" and of making observations that has allowed us to gain new empirical data as well as to reinterpret the meaning and significance of previously established data, I will start with a clinical vignette from the psychotherapy of Mrs. B. It may serve as a reference point for the discussion of the selfobject transferences.

Mrs. B. was twenty-eight years old and married when she entered treatment, fearing that she might seriously injure her two young children. She would severely beat them whenever she became uncontrollably enraged. Relatively innocuous events could precipitate these outbursts of temper. This particular symptom became much attenuated over a three-year period of her treatment. However, there remained in her a profound sense of "badness," a feeling she had had about herself all her life.

Mrs. B. had a history of severe "masochistic" acting out. She actively sought out situations where she would be assured physical suffering, such as sleeping with the windows wide open in the winter so she would freeze, and other rather bizarre forms of what may seem to the external observer as self-punishment. She had a history of severe depressions and hospitalizations following suicide attempts, but no such episodes occurred during the present treatment until the third year, when her therapist, a woman, had taken a month off from work in order to have surgery. The patient had been informed of this ahead of time.

Following a suicide attempt at this time, the patient said that she had tried to kill herself because she feared that instead of being able to depend on her therapist, in the future the therapist would have to depend on her. This course of events seemed to happen with all her friends, she said; she always ended up having to look after them.

It stood out in her background history, the therapist believed, that the patient's mother may have been psychotic. The mother was certainly not able to tolerate strong affects, neither in herself nor in her children. When upset, she would withdraw and lock herself in a closet, a circumstance which apparently occurred with some frequency. Mrs. B. remembered herself as a withdrawn and unhappy child. An early memory depicted her going into her bedroom, at age four or five, and banging her head on the floor.

The therapist reported this clinical vignette with some frustration. The problem was obviously complex: masochism, depression, suicide. The therapist was particularly distressed that the patient's depression and suicidal ideation continued even after her return from surgery and that she could not help the patient make contact with her repressed rage in the transference, although the therapist considered this essential for the prevention of further suicide attempts. The patient insisted at first that she did not feel any rage, but rather *a sense of helplessness*, which she connected with her fear that her therapist would no longer be available to her but instead would need the patient to care for *her*.

The therapist's position that it was important for Mrs. B. to face her rage then and there was a crucial one in determining the therapeutic atmosphere and further progress of the treatment. Putting the interpretive emphasis on the patient's rage was in keeping with the therapist's assumption that repressed rage was responsible for the patient's severe masochism, her temper outbursts and now, for her suicide attempt. The therapist was determined to make this unconscious affect conscious, since as long as it remained unconscious, she feared that it might still be turned against the self and acted out in the form of suicide. The patient did not respond favorably to the interpretations guided by these assumptions. The therapist saw this as an irreparable break in the therapeutic alliance. She was further distressed and puzzled about the fact that when the patient, later in the treatment, was able to feel and express her rage and haughtily withdraw from her, Mrs. B.'s depression, helplessness, and suicidal ideas did not cease. The patient had expressed her repressed, retroflected rage, so why did her symptoms not improve?

The supervisor, who was first consulted at this point, understood the situation differently: The patient's rage and emotional withdrawal from the therapist was *not* the expression of a break in the therapeutic alliance, but a disruption of what was until then a well-established, reasonably safe, protective and strength-giving relationship with a powerful, Rock-of-Gibraltar-like, reliably available therapist. It is this that in keeping with the views of Kohut we might now call a ''silent merger with an idealized selfobject'' that went unrecognized and was therefore not systematically interpreted during the first three years of treatment. The ordinary fluctuations and relatively minor disruptions of the transference prior to the therapist's surgery did not interfere with this patient's ability to experience her therapist's ongoing emotional availability. The therapist's illness, however, and her one-month absence proved a major disruption, and the patient reacted at first with helplessness, then with disappointment and rage at the traumatic loss of the therapist's ''strength and perfection.'' The therapist was now the ''sick mother'' on whom the patient could not depend. Rather, she anticipated that from now on she would have to be responsive to the therapist's needs.

It is important to note that though the therapist's surgery and absence was a repetition of the childhood trauma, the patient's reaction to the therapist was *not* a repetition of her childhood behavior. As a child she protected her mother from her rage reactions as she tried to make herself innocuous to the mother by withdrawal into isolation and loneliness—but this led the five-year-old child to engage in solitary head-bangings for self-stimulation and for alleviation of her feelings of being cut off from her mother. She was eventually able to express her rage openly at the therapist, which indicated the undoing of the childhood solution; the rage was now expressed because of the increased sense of safety that the patient had been able to establish in the three years of treatment and to reestablish a few months after the therapist's return.

As long as the therapist actively searched for hidden rage, the patient could not make contact with that feeling state. Why? For two obvious reasons: (1) The therapist pursued the rage as part of the patient's psychopathology directly, which did not yield its expected fruit—it rarely does. Only the rage that is actually mobilized in the therapist-patient relationship (even if it then remains hidden or is displaced) can be meaningfully pursued in the context of an empathic exploration of that relationship. (2) In this instance the therapist did, in fact, finally shift to an exploration of the therapeutic relationship, but did so rather suddenly after a period of three years, during which time such an exploration had not been part of their work together. The therapist's sudden interpretive attempts to "liberate" the patient's rage at her only increased the patient's self-protective efforts and her inability to feel the rage. The patient desperately needed to remain connected to the therapist, whose interventions jeopardized this very connection.

It was only when the therapist's efforts shifted toward the understanding and acknowledgment of the patient's helplessness and fear of exploitation, and to the recognition that her rage (at the loss of the therapist's protective power and at the anticipated exploitation) could not be felt, as it was potentially further disruptive, that the rage could emerge more safely and thus become part of the working through process. The therapeutic task now was to offer the patient the kind of reconstructive interpretations that would put her rage, helplessness, and despair into its current transference context, as well as into its original genetic context. The different contexts are emphasized here to indicate that the transference is not a simple repetition of the past. While the therapist's absence reactivated the childhood affects associated with the mother's vulnerability and emotional unavailability, the patient's reaction went beyond the childhood solution; she now felt free to express her rage and disappointment with the therapist, and this expression indicated her desperate need to remain in contact with the "absolute perfection" of the therapist, in order to regain and safeguard the vitality and vigor of her own psychic functioning.

The interpretation of the meaning of the disruption of the merger transference and the patient's responses to this included the reconstruction of the original circumstances in which the patient, as a child, could not express her rage without fear of further isolation from the mother. Such an emphasis on the phase-appropriateness and legitimacy of the rage and fear in the transference usually helps a patient to accept the legitimacy of a childhood demand for an accepting and responsive emotional environment. The patient then, instead of feeling contemptuous toward the enraged (bad) childhood self, can accept the frustrated child's demand for unconditional acceptance within the therapist-patient relationship. In such a relationship, with the aid of empathic reconstructive interpretations, the patient can also be aided in accepting the limitations of the therapist's "perfection," which eventually helps the patient accept the limitations of her original environment. Asking patients prematurely to accept the limitations of their original environment by calling attention to the anachronistic nature of their reactions deprives them of experiencing the "legitimacy" of their childhood wishes within the therapist-patient relationship. It is the therapist's empathy toward the angry and fearful child within the adult patient, conveyed through reconstructive interpretations that lead to insight, which the patient uses in developing her own empathy toward her original environment and her own childhood self.

This approach has to be sharply differentiated from relying on the so-called therapeutic alliance for the maintenance and completion of the working through of the transference. Working with the concept of the therapeutic alliance seems to require that the patient summon his or her adult ego capacities to distinguish between past and present, and then undo the transference distortions that inevitably enter every treatment process. From this vantage point therapists usually try to repair the strain or break in the therapeutic alliance by fostering the "real relationship," altering their own behavior, or introducing a current contextual reality external to the patient's self-experience. A preferable alternative, open to empirical study and verification, is the offering of reconstructive interpretations of the circumstances that precipitated the disruption of the selfobject transference. Such an approach would aid both the patient's cognitive grasp (i.e., it would permit the gaining of insight) and the acquisition of new psychic structures through transmuting internalizations. Herein lies the improved therapeutic leverage afforded by this approach.

I will now use this therapeutic experience with Mrs. B. to highlight the source, quality, and meaning of the selfobject transferences. These transferences unmistakably reflect as their central core the reactivation of a thwarted need to grow.

## TRANSFERENCE REACTIVATION OF THE THWARTED NEED TO GROW

We should remind ourselves briefly of the classical definition of transference, not as a solid anchoring point from which to assess our current views—such solidity is only an illusion and such assessments can be made only on the basis of careful scrutiny of the empirical data—but in order to recognize that transference has remained a slippery concept. Perhaps it will then be easier for us to consider its hitherto neglected or insufficiently noticed elements. Leites (1979) in his book, *Interpreting Transference*, documents this slipperiness with a devastating critique.

I have selected two definitions of transference —Greenson's and Kohut's—to serve as a background for our exploration. Greenson (1967) defined transference as demonstrating two outstanding characteristics: (1) it is an indiscriminate, nonselective repetition of the past; (2) it ignores or distorts reality and hence is an inappropriate reaction. Kohut's earliest definition of transference (1951) was more detailed and even then more discriminating of certain qualities of experience observed in the "psychoneuroses" and in what were then called "borderline states." He considered transference as having three components: (1) a repetitive tendency of the repressed infantile drive, (2) which is attached to old objects, (3) seeks new objects in its search for satisfaction. This was observed in the neuroses. Repetition (1) and confusion between old and new objects (2) were characteristics present in both the neuroses and the borderline states—or, as we would now say, in primary self pathology—but the third, decisive element, *the repressed drive seeking satisfaction*, is replaced in primary self pathology with a precariously balanced, fragmentation-prone self seeking reassurance. While Greenson stressed the inappropriateness of the indiscriminate, nonselective repetition of the past and the distortions of reality, Kohut explicitly included the wish for drive satisfaction in the neuroses and the wish for reassurance of the vulnerable self in self pathology. Here in this last statement is the germ of what later became the selfobject transference (Kohut, 1971, 1977).

Clinical and theoretical emphasis on the inappropriateness and distortion in the transference (on the confusion between old and new objects) rather than on its other component—the seeking of a new object for satisfaction or for reassurance (on account of the current conflictual or depleted state of the self)—has far-reaching implications for interpretation. Such an emphasis tends to invite a confrontation with reality and attempts to correct the distortion directly, however gently and tactfully. It is here, apparently, that some stalemates or transference crises occur; they are then dealt with noninterpretively, by fostering the real relationship in order to enhance the so-called therapeutic alliance and to make the patient ultimately receptive to the interpretations and reconstructions he has previously rejected.

While it is often valid that such a stalemate, especially if it occurs in patients with self pathology, may in part be due to a depletion in the analytic ambience of its minimum amount of "oxygen," we may now add that a lack of adequate comprehension of the patient's basic psychopathology, as this emerges in the transference, is a major contributing factor. This problem is not resolved analytically by fostering either the real relationship or the therapeutic alliance. This problem requires of us a comprehensive reorientation both clinically and theoretically.

What does this reorientation consist of? In the simplest sense, a sustained empathic-introspective focus on the patient's self-experience directs our attention to phenomena that make any division of the patient's experience into transference and real relationship seem an arbitrary imposition by the external observer. From within the patient's inner world, however, transference resistance, the negative therapeutic reaction, and the therapeutic alliance (among many other phenomena) take on a very different configuration, meaning, and significance. It is this new meaning and significance that the selfobject transferences reveal and encompass, both dynamically and genetically.

Dynamically, we observe that the enfeebled, vulnerable, and fragmentation-prone self is temporarily aided in reestablishing or maintaining its precarious cohesiveness with the development of a mirror transference or an idealizing transference. Genetically, both of these represent the therapeutic remobilization of infantile and childhood developmental needs, more or less phase-appropriate, that were never adequately responded to by the archaic parental selfobjects. Hence these patients were unable to acquire self-assertive ambitions on the one hand, and internalized values and ideals on the other, through the transmuting internalization of the functions of their selfobjects. Lifelong efforts to defensively cover the void, to strengthen the acquired compensatory structures, or to search for selfobjects in the hope of completing their arrested development, can be readily observed in these patients. In the transference, if things go well, the strengthening of the compensatory structures will lead to necessary structure-building through transmuting internalization of the therapist's selfobject functions rather than through identifications.

Returning to the clinical vignette of Mrs. B., our usual assumption would be that we have succeeded in reviving aspects of her central psychopathology, especially the dis-

torted perception that the therapist has become as emotionally unavailable to her as was her mother. But can we now
see how her particular transference also represents, perhaps
even more forcefully, *a reactivation of her thwarted need
to grow*? More particularly, can we recognize that her experience of improved psychic functioning in a relatively
undisturbed merger with the strength and power of the therapist reflected her revived ability to silently borrow from
her idealized selfobject-therapist what she had been unable
to acquire in infancy and childhood? And does it not follow
that the subsequent major disruption of her functioning and
the emergence of her helplessness, depression, and suicide
attempt were the consequences of the traumatic rupture of
this selfobject transference that *repeated* that original trauma
with her mother and was therefore not simply a distorted
revival of it?

The answers to these questions lead us more deeply into
a reexamination of Mrs. B.'s psychopathology than we may
have originally anticipated. Her masochism and depression
will take on a different cast. Mrs. B.'s childhood solution
to the emotional unavailability of her mother was to suffer
silently and to withdraw from her, since her mother herself
would become intolerably agitated and instead of calming
Mrs. B. would make things worse by closeting herself away
from her child when she was most needed. Mrs. B.'s silent
withdrawal and the solitary head-banging for self-stimulation, her childhood solution to feeling cut off from a desperately needed selfobject, was now in the transference
slowly overcome by focusing on what was becoming a new
mode of relating, rather than primarily or exclusively on the
repetitive aspects of the transference. Mrs. B., through her
growing ability to express her rage directly in the transference in response to its various and repetitive disruptions,
was thereby able to establish a living, intense—though angry—bond between herself and her therapist. This did in-

deed represent the effort in the transference to resume a thwarted growth. The point to emphasize here is that psychic growth or structure-building, whether in childhood or in psychotherapy or psychoanalysis, can occur only within an empathically responsive selfobject milieu. When in treatment the disruptions of a silent merger with the idealized therapist bring forth rage and destructive feelings or fantasies, the patient experiences the therapist differently from the original selfobject, the mother. If the therapist is indeed capable of *not* experiencing himself as the target of the patient's rages and can retain his focus on the patient's subjective experience, he will be able to offer a reconstructive interpretation that will "legitimize" the rage within the transference. Such an interpretation, then, not only helps to reestablish the merger transference but also helps the patient accept the demands of his or her childhood self.

We may now ask what aspects of our theory of the transference (and the nature of psychopathology) and what aspects of our therapeutic techniques might have interfered with the clearer recognition of the presence and significance of this unextinguished developmental thrust or thwarted need to complete a derailed or interrupted growth. Could it be that our emphasis on the indiscriminate repetitions and distortions, on the inappropriateness of these reactions—that is, our near exclusive focus upon pathology—blocked our vision and interfered with our proper appraisal of the role and function of this thwarted need to grow, which is the motive force of the selfobject transference and of the therapeutic work within it? The need to complete the unfinished business of psychological growth and maturation is a stronger force and ally in therapy than we had previously been able to recognize. Could it be that we have taken the inevitability of repetition—the fact that we always approach each new situation with our repertoire of past modes of coping—and have inferred from this that there was a ubiquitous, hard-to-combat *compulsion* to repeat? Could this have made us less sensitive to a more profound "dread to repeat" (Ornstein, 1974) and to the incessant search for a new beginning? Could it be, we may further ask, that we have overgeneralized from certain clinical observations in which elaborate archaic defensive structures make it difficult or impossible for the patient, for quite some time, to accept and make use of the analyst's empathy and, therefore, to dare revive this thwarted developmental need to grow?

My own answers to all of these questions are in the affirmative. The interpretive focus on what the patient is searching for (what might seem to the *external* observer as mere repetition of the past), on what had been originally traumatically interrupted and had derailed his psychological growth, and on what might block its resumption in the transference would lead ultimately to a more or less extensive remobilization of the traumatically frustrated needs of infancy and childhood. This, in turn, would prepare the opportunity for belated acquisition of psychic structures within the bipolar self.

## REFERENCES

Freud, S. (1900), The Interpretation of Dreams. *Standard Edition*, 4–5. London: Hogarth Press, 1953.
——— (1905), Fragment of an analysis of a case of hysteria. *Standard Edition*, 7:7–122. London: Hogarth Press, 1953.
Greenson, R.R. (1967), *The Technique and Practice of Psychoanalysis*. New York: International Universities Press.
Kohut, H. (1951), Discussion of "The function of the analyst in the therapeutic process" by Samuel D. Lipton. In: *The Search for the Self*, Vol. 1, ed. P. Ornstein. New York: International Universities Press, pp. 159–166.
——— (1971), *The Analysis of the Self*. New York: International Universities Press.
——— (1977), *The Restoration of the Self*. New York: International Universities Press.
Leites, N. (1979), *Interpreting Transference*. New York: Norton.

Ornstein, A. (1974), The dread to repeat and the new beginning: A contribution to the psychoanalysis of narcissistic personality disorders. *Annual of Psychoanalysis*, 2:231–248. New York: International Universities Press.

# 5

# Discussion

Question 1: *Please comment on the apparent conflict be-tween Dr. Valenstein's comment that in preoedipal trans-ference it is the doing, and not the talking, that is important, and Dr. Ornstein's example in which it was the talking—the transference interpretation—that complicated the therapy.*

*Ornstein*: I think it's a good thing that this central issue comes up so early, and I welcome the opportunity to hear from Dr. Valenstein as to how he would elaborate his po-sition after hearing my disagreement with the view that it is more the doing than the talking.

The notion that the doing is more important is, by the way, pervasive in the psychoanalytic literature. Balint cer-tainly felt that under certain circumstances at least a sym-bolic doing was necessary. You may recall that he had described this in relation to one of his patients who wanted to touch him. He did let the patient touch one of his fingers, which was only a momentary doing, after he had tried all the interpretations of which he could think. After that touch-ing, the patient was able to relate to Balint differently and thus had a chance for a "new beginning" (1932) in the treatment process. Balint based his understanding and his approach on the idea that narcissistic disorders inevitably originate in the earliest, the most archaic period of devel-opment.

Kohut made a decisive departure from this assumption when he developed the idea of a line of development for narcissism separate from that for object love. This immediately brought to the fore the notion that problems of the sort we are talking about—and that Dr. Valenstein has focused on beautifully in his descriptions both here and elsewhere—do not necessarily originate in the preverbal sphere. Even when they do, there may be a reverberation in those deeper, preverbal layers, of verbal interventions, through the so-called telescoping of events. In other words, one can talk to people about those earlier experiences in the language of later experience—into which the earlier ones may have been telescoped—in such a way that they feel profoundly understood; they respond to this viscerally, as though throughout their whole being. Therefore I feel that we ought to take every chance we have to explore and to understand—to communicate this understanding, and when appropriate, to offer explanations. As I said earlier, we first have to accept what is brought to us, including the so-called extraordinary demands, the egoistic perceptions, and the wish to dominate the therapeutic scene. Note how all of this is usually described in the external observer's judgmental language and refers to those "unacceptable" patterns we think we need to alter in our patients' attitudes and behavior. In psychoanalytic psychotherapy we should *accept* them, *understand* them, and ultimately *interpret* them.

Understanding is provided on both a verbal and a nonverbal level, simultaneously. I think we should try to raise such understanding, whenever possible, to the level of verbally expressible insights. Now here is an empirical issue rather than a theoretical or conceptual or, let us say, an a priori bias. We could make use of such verbal interventions that we now have available as a result of the expansion of contemporary psychoanalysis to see if these interventions do indeed allow patients to feel better understood, to gain insight into these so-called narcissistic issues, and then to see finally whether they actually respond more favorably.

*Valenstein*: Analysis is not just a therapy; it's also a mode of understanding things which cannot always be directly translated into a therapeutic approach. A one-to-one matching would be a mistake, in my opinion. The therapeutic issue of endless repeating, rather than remembering, goes back to Ferenczi, who actually encouraged reenactment within the transference situation for those stalemated instances when remembering on a verbal level failed, and when explanation, that is, interpretation, had very limited results. The account of Balint's symbolic finger-touching is very much in keeping with Ferenczi's approach. The issue is that, of course one talks sense to a patient; you don't just talk 'ball game.' The question is what is really decisive hierarchically in inducing the change. To what extent *really* is there structure building and to what extent is there secondary elaboration of what I would call latter-day accessions to earlier distresses and disturbances? I raise the question as to whether in the reeducative ambience and atmosphere (reeducative in the broader and not in the pedantic sense), in the capsule of mutual understanding, there is a kind of recrudescence or regrowth of what had been deficient. Some French analysts practically make a mystique of this aspect of the therapeutic endeavor—this therapeutic centrum of an almost ideally, perfectly mutual, empathically understood setting in which the unconscious understands the unconscious. It sounds a little like hypnosis to me, but identifying these matters is the vehicle which lends sense and prescience to what is remembered, namely, the affect prescience—the affects with their associated psychomotor and psychovisceral referents, those earliest memory traces that are not laid down in discrete memories. Explanations addressed to these latter are reconstructions, in my opinion—necessary reconstructions but reconstructions nonetheless—with all their uses and limitations. They are not actually the original experience in the way that we understand postverbal experience out of the photographic memory book of specific pictures. The articulate explanations that are addressed to these reconstructions are addressed to the secondary, tertiary, and later successive aspects which pick up the valence of the early attachments, including the evolving sense of self-sufficiency and self-esteem—thus implying the very earliest time developmentally, one which cannot be exactly remembered.

*Michels*: It seems to me that there are important areas of agreement between Drs. Ornstein and Valenstein, which I will first focus on before commenting upon the narrow area of disagreement between them.

I think they both agree that all interpretive or therapeutic activity has important meaning, both at the cognitive, secondary-process content level, and inevitably—no matter who the patient or what the nature of the intervention—at earlier, more primitive, more preverbal, more experiential levels as well. Further, both of these are always present.

Secondly, I think they agree that the relative importance of these two types of meaning varies from patient group to patient group. In general, the earlier the sources of the major themes of psychopathology in developmental terms, the closer the patient is to borderline or narcissistic categories rather than structural or conflictual (that is, neurotic) categories, the more important the less symbolic aspects of the interpretive process would be. I believe that Dr. Ornstein would agree that this is true.

It seems to me that they also agree that insight, understanding, and cognitive comprehension are never total in any patient in any treatment, or in any type of pathology. Accepting these three themes of argreement, the disagreement appears to be about their relative therapeutic optimism or nihilism in the treatment of sicker, more disturbed patients, and the extent to which the meaningful content of the interpretation, in contrast to its other aspects, contributes to its therapeutic effect. This may focus the difference a bit; it helps me to understand it, at least.

Question 2: *In the case of Mrs. B., would you, Dr. Michels, have dealt with the transference issue or let it remain silent over three years? If you had chosen to bring it to light in the therapy, how would you have done it? Would this in your opinion have prevented the events occurring after the therapist's surgery?*

*Dr. Michels*: I have trouble with the description of the treatment of Dr. Ornstein's patient. I would not have treated the patient the way the therapist did in the first place—nor, of course, would Dr. Ornstein have. This is not because the therapist's theory of psychopathology was right or wrong, but because there was a dramatic error in the understanding of how one conducts treatment—an error which I believe has to do with an overinterest in theory rather than in *which* theory one is overinterested. As I understand the description of the case, a therapist interpreted a patient's affect without any evidence that the affect was present—without any clinical suggestion that it was there, or even that it was lurking under the surface, was preconscious, that there were hints of it, or that there were derivatives of it—but rather because the therapist had read an article that suggested that this particular pattern was associated with that affect. Based on that theory and deductions from it, an interpretation was made of the patient's experience in the treatment setting. That is not psychotherapy; it is something else, regardless of what the theory is. An equally severe error would have been making an interpretation of a selfobject transference based on having read an article by Dr. Ornstein; or, having attended this conference and then seeing a similar patient, making an interpretation without any clinical evidence that the phenomenon was present. That is the core problem, it seems to me. The other problems are all derivative.

Moving on to the question I was asked—What would I have done with this patient?—I think the answer does not depend upon whether one accepts Dr. Ornstein's theory or the theory of whomever it is Dr. Ornstein may be arguing with here, but rather on what happened clinically in those three years. There was no clinical evidence that this patient was using the relationship with the therapist in order to stabilize a concern about the "fragmentation" of an inadequately "cohesive self" (to use the language of self psychology). I do not believe that can go on for three years without derivatives that can be detected in the clinical data. Therefore the question isn't whether or not one would interpret it, but if there were derivatives, what would one do with them? That depends on the treatment, its goals, its intensity, the nature of the contract as open-ended or closed-ended, the pathology that brings the patient to treatment, the therapist's capacity to deal with that kind of material, the risk of negative effects of that kind of intervention, the capacity of the treatment situation to deal with those negative effects, the other life circumstances of the patient, and all the things that go into such a clinical judgment. I believe the answer in some situations would be that you would actively pursue such clues and explore them. The answer in other situations would be that you would ignore such clues unless they presented major resistances to pursuing the specific goals of treatment—and I believe Dr. Ornstein would agree with that.

*Ornstein*: I largely would. Dr. Michels recognizes the fact that there are many issues to consider in this treatment process. One of them is the educational—the general idea of how to do psychotherapy. I agree with the idea that no theory would have helped if it were imposed on the clinical data. This particular therapist—sensitive as she was, and theoretically not unsophisticated, but perhaps not very adept at this stage at bringing theories to bear in a useful way upon the clinical process—was doing what she called "supportive psychotherapy." She may even have thought that the "drive-defense" interpretations she tried early on drove the patient to distraction and therefore would have been less helpful. She therefore became noninterpretive, relatively quiet, and as a result, in her description of the first three years of tratment, failed to recognize at the time—though she did so retrospectively—what had transpired during those years. What then emerged, however, was that after the rupture in the transference she was still searching for those affects she thought were part of the psychopathology. When that didn't work she had the good sense to seek supervision. It was at that point that we had an idea—perhaps jointly developed—of what the first three years were all about, how much they indeed contributed to what she was able to do subsequently (after she returned from surgery) with the patient.

Now, about the various theories: Clearly, this case does not lend itself, because of those first three years, to sort out all the problems we have with the various theories about the nature of the transference. One thing, however, is obvious: transference, unless its disruptions are recognized, is very hard to deal with interpretively. I agree with Dr. Michels that there were, retrospectively, evidences of the presence of minor disruptions which should have been dealt with. I don't know whether in Dr. Valenstein's approach the search for interpretive or noninterpretive responses to the transference would have hinged upon its minor or temporary disruptions. I am very curious about how he would have dealt with it. I could deal with it most effectively only in terms of the disruptions. It is therefore an important issue that one can interpretively deal with it, if one has a conception of the nature of the experience within an archaic or not-so-archaic selfobject transference. We don't have the linguistic capabilities—the ability to translate that experience into a language than can be communicated—if we don't have a notion of what that cohesive transference is. Otherwise, we might be able to interpret bits of the experience, based upon developmental ideas. This relates to Dr. Schwaber's question: what can we do with observational data we get from infant researchers; how can we transport those back into the transference? I would answer to the latter part of the question: only with a great deal of difficulty and uncertainty.

*Schwaber*: I think it is striking, though not surprising, that our discussion tends to pivot around the clinical example.

If we consider Dr. Michels' comment about the over-interest in theory, the question might be raised, was it Freud's use of the theoretical model that he had at the time in treating Dora—the crossing through a repression barrier from the unconscious to the preconscious—that led him to overlook the transference? Or, put another way, was it his capacity to transcend the theory which permitted him to reconsider what *else* he may have heard from the patient that was meaningful about her treatment?

In asking Dr. Valenstein to respond to Dr. Ornstein's comments, I shall include the next submitted question.

Question 3: *To what extent does psychoanalytic technique depend on psychoanalytic theory? And to what extent is psychoanalytic theory an explanatory elaboration or articulation of what seems to work? Doesn't the latter imply the possibility of a radically different, scientifically revolution-*

*ary reconception which would not greatly affect clinical
work analogous to the way the Einsteinian revolution didn't
affect air flight? What might such a reconception look like?
In other words, what are the axioms of psychoanalytic theory and what might they be?*

*Schwaber*: This question again brings to focus the issue of
the relationship between theoretical model and technique.

*Valenstein*: I think it's a point well taken—the implications
of the question whether one should seek a one-to-one correspondence between theory and practice. The fact that
something works doesn't entitle anybody necessarily to offer
a theory which is close to his or her heart as the basis for
a technical success. That's one of the great errors, that
technical success gives one the privilege of introducing a
new theory. It may be that it worked clinically for quite a
different reason. Success in itself confers no license. Nonetheless, it's useful to try to find what in theory is close to
the clinical situation, what is heuristic, and what serves until
something better comes along. There may have been things
from before that were already useful and sufficient; one
doesn't have to spin a whole new nosology and a new
theory. I think this is partially the controversy over Kohut's
contributions, which are stimulating, just as the Kleinians
had a very stimulating set of clinical observations to bring
forward; but I certainly think a lot of Kleinian theory was
mythology. True, if they could share it with their patients
indisputably, emphatically in a dedicated fashion, to the
enhancement of an omnipotent umbrella transference situation for people who are frail and uncertain of their own
competence—within such a transference they could have
a great deal of therapeutic impact. I do not, however, believe
that gave them the option of coining a set of impressions
as to what happens sophisticatedly in the first year of life;

some of their constructions, to my mind, were highly adul-
tomorphic and very peripheral. To some extent, the same
question arises out of Kohut's contributions as to whether
the clinical material that is offered necessarily validates the
theory that is suggested along with it. So the question is
quite in order.

To go back to some of the other issues, I think there is
a difference between the congruence of cognitive verbal
referents in a later phase of development and in an earlier
phase. I think this issue is reflected also in some of the
ambiguities that come up around material such as Dr. Ornstein has presented, and such as has been described in some
of the Kohut case descriptions, where it is said sometimes—and I couldn't agree more—that it is very hard to
deal interpretively with very early transference affect. Deal
interpretively means *mutatively*, in Strachey's sense of the
word—to catch hold of the experiential, what I call the
*erlebnis*, the inner emotional reliving which carries a sense
of the affect and some prescience for elusive events that are
vague and obscure, and essentially beyond recollection.
They may have been validated, or at least scored by later
recollections and once-removed historical data provided by
others.

As an example: a patient of mine, who I think showed
both qualities of transference—one, the issue of trust/mistrust
on an early level, and then, the structural oedipal aspects
of this, superimposed upon the earlier—told me that from
the age of six months to a year and a half, having been born
with a congenital defect in her lower limbs, she was put in
a brace greatly restricting her mobility. She also had a
mother whom we knew from later events was limitedly
perceptive and limitedly sensitive in her response to children, and even less so to infants. We extrapolated the prob-
ability that this mother did not meet the child's needs for
adequate connectedness. The patient had also had nannies
who appeared to have been similarly limited. Thus she had

the combination of a trauma plus, which we knew historically.

All that this patient remembered was one occasion when
the bedclothes were lifted so that she could pull her limbs
onto the mattress in order to lie flat in bed, and how awkward
it was for her. But she had certain affect predilection, when
stressfully confronted, to fall into a state of consternation,
dismay, massive anxiety, and massive distress, which she
felt probably connected with this situation of having been
bound down, and under circumstances where there was a
great deal of affective isolation. We thereby reconstructed
something in that regard. She was a woman who looked for
explanations and was quite thoughtful. We talked about the
probabilities in her development and the deficits which then
were repeated, in terms that can be remembered from three
and four years on. She brought me a picture showing herself
at age three, posing in this rather stiff stylized way. She
said, "I know it's me because of the way I'm holding my
hands, and it reminds me of how I probably felt because
I have felt that way as long as I know, under certain circumstances."

We could address the later reference interpretively; we
could speculate reconstructively with a strong sense of its
probably having been so for the earlier paradigm situations.
It made sense to her, offering a likely explanatory chain to
what had probably taken place very early in her development. The issue of the transference aspects, however, being
very closely, very experientially known in the here and now,
when linked to the then and there, was more fuzzy for the
early years than for the later.

I am usually hesitant to talk of structure building in the
original sense rather than in the secondary elaborated sense
of what happens postverbally.

*Schwaber*: We can see here the continuing reflection on this
issue of what experiences within the clinical situation can

be brought into focus in the interpretive process. Is there a whole realm of experiences that have therapeutic impact but do not reach levels of cognition or awareness, that can usefully be addressed, interpretively? Of course, implicitly, this brings us back to the earlier question—can interpretations be brought to bear on levels of experience which do touch on preoedipal developmental issues, and, if not, how can we specifically address these issues?

*Ornstein*: I would like to respond to a very important issue that Dr. Valenstein has raised. Psychoanalysts are in a difficult position from an epistemological point of view to know what it is that can allow us to introduce theories and what it is that supports our conservative sense of maintaining what we have inherited. Of course, this is put into the extreme because Freudian theory has been slowly and continuously modified over the years; there has been no standstill in that regard. But certain modifications allow and are designed to maintain the basic structure even when clinical evidence suggests that our clinical theories no longer help us with many—and some people would even say with most—of our patients. In other words, if we do not restrict our choice to the classic neurotic patients, we do seem to run into a great deal of trouble. The question is, do we run into trouble because our theories do not allow us—or do not buttress—our empathic perceptions and our interpretive capabilities, or is it for other reasons?

We are accustomed to blaming patients for certain difficulties in relation to their unanalyzability, or even in relation to their "untherapizability"—to coin, for momentary use, a rather infelicitous term. Could we, at least for experimental purposes, without violating our basic assumptions, go back to Dora, as an example, to reconsider some of these questions? Dora is a paradigmatic case; there's no doubt about it. Freud's analysis of Dora, no matter what we think of that analysis now, is historically brilliant and, in that sense, lasting. But did Freud really listen to Dora? Did Freud really understand Dora? Many people have said—and documented it beautifully—that Freud, while he elaborated the concept of transference retrospectively on the experience with Dora, did not listen to, did not hear, and did not understand Dora—whereupon Dora picked up and left. To argue retrospectively, as Freud did, that it was the lack of recognition of the transference that made Dora leave, would lead to the conclusion that he had postulated a theory—a clinical theory—and thought he had proven it through her analysis, which was, in any event, only a fragment of an analysis. Given all these problems, can we legitimately retain the Dora analysis as anything other than a most remarkable historical document from whose methodology we can continually learn but whose data and results we cannot use without drastic alterations? Were we to have a contemporary Dora, would we not be entitled, on the basis of successes with her, to alter our theories, or should we say, as Dr. Valenstein apparently is suggesting, that, after all, since there is no direct one-to-one relationship between theory and technique, we should analyze the new Dora the way we think we could understand her better and then leave our theories untouched? This, to me, does not make epistemological sense.

I think we are entitled to seek new ways of extracting from clinical experiences what we need for building a theory that will more directly lead us to the understanding of our patients. On this matter, I have a long-standing disagreement with Dr. Michels, who has a more relativistic notion about theory and perhaps, therefore, does not look to the clinical data for a confirmation of the validity of the theory, nor vice versa. He sees theory here and clinical experience there, with some relationship, undoubtedly—but I don't know how to characterize that relationship from his vantage point. It seems to me that to come up with new ideas for theories, one first has to be more committed to the theory one is using than Dr. Michels is willing to be—although I would go in his direction a long step by saying that I use theories simply and merely as tools of observation. When my tools of observation no longer allow me to see clearly and organize my clinical data encompassingly enough, then I need new tools in order to enhance my capacity to organize my data and see things better. It is in this regard that I do not feel that Dr. Valenstein did justice to the new ideas that have been presented by Kohut on self psychology, for it is precisely this opportunity to transcend the limits of what we could observe clinically before that Kohut has offered us with his new theories.

*Schwaber*: I will ask Dr. Michels to respond, while also considering the next question.

Question 4: *Could you elaborate on the meaning of myths? What is the impact on the patient's treatment, of considering the patient's perceptions as myth rather than as a history of genesis, as Dr. Michels suggests?*[1]

*Michels*: Myth and theory questions to me are closely related. There are many roles of theory in psychoanalysis. That it plays an important sociological role you've seen evidence of in this panel, as turf is staked out with theoretical mileposts. It plays an important developmental role, as therapists use theories as transitional objects in their own development when they move from working in close association

---

[1]Dr. Michels raises this idea in response to Dr. Schwaber's sixth introductory question.

with their mentors to therapeutic autonomy in their work with patients.

Pasteur said—in talking about scientific inquiry—that chance favors the prepared mind. Theory prepares the analyst's or therapist's mind so that a theoretically informed therapist hears and sees things differently, comprehends them differently, and therefore responds to them differently. It seems to me clearly wrong—and I'm sure Dr. Ornstein would edit it out of his script—to say that Freud did not understand Dora. Freud had a brilliant understanding of Dora. There are other understandings of Dora in addition to Freud's. Freud recognized in his postscript that some of the understandings he did not have at a critical junction in the treatment became the limiting factors in its success. No one ever totally understands anyone. No theory of human behavior is complete or comprehensive. However, our theories give us a variety of ways of understanding people. The history of psychoanalysis has been of growth in the breadth and plurality of its theories, so that more and more patients can be comprehended from multiple frames of reference and points of view. From time to time in various cases, with various patients, one or the other of those theories may help us to understand the limiting factors in a treatment. To use all points of view at all times with all patients indiscriminately is to guarantee almost always being irrelevant to the patient. The skill is to know which one to use at which time, and that's a science that doesn't yet exist. Unfortunately, in practice, the choice of theory usually depends more on the schooling of the therapist than on the clinical problem being confronted in the treatment. I believe we may be making some early moves toward addressing that question, but they're very early.

Myth is to me a dignified term that has no pejorative connotations; in fact, quite the contrary. Myths are among the most noble creations of civilization; they are works of art; they are articulated and eloquent entities that embody the central meanings of societies. Freud talked of myths that way. I once debated a man who had used the word ''myth'' as a pejorative attack on the concept of mental illness. My position in that debate was that he had made an error, not in saying that mental illness was a myth, but in being over-optimistic about the social status of psychiatric concepts. Mental illness is *almost* a myth in our society, but it has not yet achieved that level of significance in our culture.

I believe that our theories are myths, as are our genetic reconstructions. That means they are vital tools for comprehending and understanding our experience as clinicians, our patients' experiences in their lives, and for helping them to integrate and organize those experiences into structures that serve as the frameworks for their continuing lives. That is what a myth does for a culture; that is what a genetic myth does for a patient. Myths are not irrelevant to the veridical historical facts, but they don't simply reflect those facts. They are the products of a creative process that draws upon those facts. I think that that is what we do in our genetic reconstructions. I think that they are only distantly related to the observational, developmental, and fascinating data of the baby watchers. Our patients come to us because their current myths aren't working well, and we help them reconstruct and construct new myths. In doing so, we draw on our theoretical myths and on the presumptive developmental histories which are the way that patients and some analysts generally label the genetic myths they reconstruct, as Dr. Schwaber did in her introduction. That would be, to me, the relationship between theory, myth, and development.

*Valenstein*: I think the term ''relativistic'' is the one that appeals to me most. It isn't that anything stands still; it was always said that practice influences theory, and theory influences practice, but not that there was a one-to-one correspondence between them. You have to test one against the other for as much useful approximation as is possible, and watch the historical chronology and curve as you go, to retain what is economically conservative, historically useful, and still heuristic, so to speak, and to attach to it additional increments—whether from practice or from theory. I never had in mind that one's practice is intuitively changing according to clinical recognitions, while theories stand absolutely removed and still. I couldn't possibly think that. But I am very thoughtful about what theoretical implications I draw from my clinical experience, and rather cautious about what clinical implications or applications I draw from theory.

*Ornstein*: I wanted to respond to Dr. Michels' suggestion that if I had a chance to edit the script, I would delete my remark that Freud didn't understand Dora. No, I would like to *underline* that Freud did not understand Dora; he *explained* her. And his explanations at present are questionable.

If Freud would have understood Dora and responded to her from within the vantage point of that understanding rather than from within the vantage point of proving his theory or articulating it, he would have recognized that foremost in the transference was Dora's demand—a very peremptory demand—that he, Freud, should understand that Dora's father, in a certain way had really mistreated her by pushing her toward Mr. K. and thereby maintaining his liaison with Mrs. K. This was not interpretively encompassed and it was not included in the theoretical formulations that the Dora experience actually demands us to do now, retrospectively.

*Schwaber*: We come to our conclusion on the question of

the relativity of theory and of the nature of the relationship between theory and practice. Theory is an essential clinical tool and yet may also be an impediment to clinical discovery. To rephrase the question I had earlier asked in the case of Dora: Was it that the theoretical model Freud held at that time interfered with his ability to hear the transference implications in the clinical process, or was it his not yet having elaborated a theory of transference which kept him from noting its vicissitudes within Dora's experience?

Perhaps the creative leap for each of us might occur at a moment in which we are able to transcend our theoretical model to hear something new or different. Then we may return to the model, using our discovery to elaborate or refine it.

REFERENCE

Balint, M. (1932), Character analysis and new beginning. In: *Primary Love and Psychoanalytic Technique*, sec. ed. London: Tavistock Publications & New York: Liveright Publishing Co., 1965.

# Part II

# 6

# Preoedipal Influences Reflected in the Transference, with Special Reference to Women

ELEANOR GALENSON, M.D.

Although it is now generally agreed that the findings of infant observational research will cast light on adult psychopathology and treatment, and help clarify the contribution of preoedipal experiences to transference manifestations and their management in psychoanalytic as well as in psychotherapeutic treatment, the specific forms in which these early experiences manifest themselves and their optimal management remain the subject of considerable debate. For one, the remnants of these early eras are readily confused with reflections of later experiences appearing in more regressive forms.

My approach to the problem has evolved from my parallel experiences of carrying out infant research and engaging in the psychoanalytic and psychotherapeutic treatment of adults over the past twenty-five years. Familiarity with specific patterns and characteristics of preoedipal psychological organization derived from work with infants has proven invaluable as a framework from which to consider aspects of transference manifestations in adult patients presenting a similar type of organization. I shall suggest that such similarities can be clinically useful in both analytic and psychotherapeutic work with adult patients.

The form in which preoedipal material is reflected in the transference will be illustrated by describing clinical data derived from the treatment of a female patient during a period when the transference was characterized by homosexual wishes and painful feelings of shame. These began to emerge as the termination of a lengthy psychoanalytic treatment was being considered by the patient for the first time. I shall attempt to demonstrate the genetic and organizational connection between particular aspects of the transference, her homosexual wishes and feelings of shame, and vivid infantile memories of painful states of sexual arousal along with early fears vaguely related to feelings of genital inadequacy and severe temper tantrums. These three elements comprise a constellation which coincides in form, pattern of drive organization, and defensive structure with the constellation of behaviors which Roiphe and I have observed in girls during the preoedipal era of life in connection with their early sexual arousal and discoveries (Galenson and Roiphe, 1976; Roiphe and Galenson, 1982). As we found in some of the girls in our research study, the mother of my patient had used her young child in a particularly narcissistic manner, which appeared to have aroused premature and excessive sexual tension as well as anger. Both of these states were only partially discharged through temper tantrums, and my patient recalled a rather constant background state of sexual arousal that often led to excessive masturbation. This particular type of mother-child interaction differs from the usual, more soothing type, although both contain elements of erotic interchange which I believe characterize all early mother-child relationships. Finally, I shall describe another pattern which seems preoedipal in nature as it appeared in the transference—a pattern characterized by sudden regressive shifts of state and mood which are similar to those seen during the first year or two of infancy. This tendency toward sudden regression and recovery is, I believe, more common in women than in men, and is possibly due to the greater persistence in women of the preoedipal tie to the mother.

## CASE MATERIAL

Returning to treatment after the summer vacation, this middle-aged female patient began her first session by relating a dream in which she was standing and looking down at a man in bed who at first resembled her husband. In the dream, she became intensely aroused genitally as she stood there, and then she joined the man in bed. However, she was sexually dissatisfied when the man made a few penile thrusts into her vagina. Then the man was replaced by the patient's adolescent son, whom she pulled down to lie on top of her. Upon awakening, she felt sexually aroused and somewhat anxious, feelings which persisted throughout the day. She said she was startled by the overt sexual feelings in the dream, which she associated to her father, and she remembered, as she had on previous occasions, that he had always been physically demonstrative to her and to the rest of the family. She also again recalled the belief she had held since her adolescence that she had been born with an insatiable degree of sexual desire which had *antedated* any sexual strivings felt toward her father. Then she mentioned for the first time that she now suspected that it was her beloved nursemaid (who had left during my patient's eighteenth month, just after the birth of her baby brother) who was really responsible, by having deliberately caressed her charge's genitals, for this early and distressing sexual arousal.

Although my patient had no actual memory of any such

incident, her sense of conviction that it had indeed occurred came from an experience she now related to me for the first time; it was one which had continued to arouse unusually intense shame and embarrassment whenever she had thought of it and as she now related it during the analytic session. (Until now, neither shame nor embarrassment had played important roles during her several years of treatment with me.) This was the episode she related: while diapering a friend's baby girl during the previous winter, she had felt compelled to stroke the infant's genitals and had been aware of her own simultaneous feelings of sexual arousal. However, she controlled the impulse and had merely stroked the inner aspects of the infant's thighs and briefly touched her genitals. The incident had left her bewildered and deeply ashamed, and only now, about a year later, could she relate it to me. The experience and its accompanying sexual arousal reminded her of exploratory "under-the-cover sexual looking" games she had played with several female peers during latency. She then described another "shameful" experience, one which had also been too painful to describe until now. One of her many masturbatory fantasies was unlike all the others in that it was not only the most exciting but was also the only one involving other women; the fantasy consisted of being stroked genitally by an older woman. This reminded her of the older women in a book she had recently read who prepared the younger girls for their careers as prostitutes by stimulating their genitals tenderly and gently. Although my patient always found this fantasy extremely stimulating, paradoxically, it led to feeling quietly contented rather than to any orgastic culmination.

The material of this first hour differed from our prior work together in several ways. As my patient now acknowledged, she had become aware of erotic feelings toward me for the first time as she described to me the fantasy of being masturbated by older women. She was upset by these feelings, since overt erotic feelings toward women had never been consciously experienced before; she then related how eager she had been to see me again this fall. She had felt more tender and loving toward me, but felt ashamed and embarrassed as she described this change in attitude. Neither the tender love for women nor intense shame had ever before appeared in a distinct and conscious form in her everyday life or in the transference relationship.

Some changes had occurred during my patient's recent summer vacation. In contrast to previous ones, she had often consciously thought of wanting to share her sense of growing enjoyment in her femaleness with me, femaleness which seemed to have both sexual and nonsexual components. She had also become much more aware of herself as an individual, apart from her husband and children, and she had decided to take an important step professionally which would of necessity modify her current family arrangements. Of particular significance was the fact that this professional step would lead to a gradual decrease in the frequency of her analytic sessions and the beginning of her separation from me.

The clinical material and its transference implications can be understood in part as follows: While the overt dream material was obviously concerned with oedipal wishes, her associations quickly moved to preoedipal experiences, perhaps in part as a regressive defense. However, the major dynamic force appeared to be the threat of the impending "separation for good" and the reflections of the more archaic aspect of the transference, delineating her preoedipal attachment to her mother.

Although much ground concerning her relationship with her mother had already been traversed during our previous work, we now explored some of its early components relating to renewed fears of separation (a line of investigation which would be appropriate to psychotherapy as well as to psychoanalytic treatment). The patient remembered her mother's sexual exhibitionism when she drank heavily and danced and sang in public, alternating with contrasting states of inhibition during which she withdrew into sobriety and excessive modesty, involving both herself and her children. My patient also again recalled her severe childhood temper tantrums, the subject of frequent discussions during previous years of treatment, but now with newly emergent associations indicating that the tantrums served as a means of discharge for unbearable *sexual tension*, as well as anger. The tantrums were often precipitated by some interchange between her younger brother and her mother in which they seemed to somehow instigate my patient's many acutely shameful and embarrassing experiences. These episodes had been linked with a vague sense of genital incompetency and would inevitably lead to anger as well as sexual arousal. Both affects would then be discharged through temper tantrums and urination. The same sequence of sexual arousal, the feeling of being exposed as genitally incompetent, followed by anger and then the explosion in tantrums and urination, constituted the elements of many of her masturbatory fantasies during her latency, adolescence, and adulthood; they were consciously recalled as having appeared for the first time during her fifth year, and they remained a source of secret shame during her years of analysis until their final emergence after the dream about her father.

Other archaic elements of the transference also appeared for the first time following the dream, but were reflected in her relationship with her husband. (The analytic process allowed for this more extensive exploration, while psychotherapy might have offered less of an opportunity.) Their sexual adjustment was a moderately satisfactory one, but now my patient began to feel sexually aroused precisely at those times when her husband was either upset or particularly fatigued, and predictably uninterested in sex. His "rebuffs" at this time led to a recurrence of my patient's severe insomnia states during which she prowled about the house in a state of sexual arousal, exactly as she remembered her insomniac nights of childhood. She felt at the mercy of her intense sexual feelings, as masturbation to relieve the sexual tension brought on the sadomasochistic fantasies she had always avoided whenever possible.

During this period of treatment, my patient's struggle over sexual arousal, shame, frustration, and its final angry and urinary release reminded me every so often of many of the little girls of fifteen to twenty-four months whom Roiphe and I had observed during the course of our research. We described the reactions of these infants to their emerging genital sexuality and their sense of sexual identity, as they compared themselves genitally with the genitals of their fathers, male peers, and other males they saw. Among the typical sequences were those in which eighteen- or nineteen-month-old girls urinated on the floor of the nursery, and as the urinary stream ran down between diaper and thigh and puddled on the floor, the infants looked startled as they gazed down at the puddle. They then blushed deeply and ran to their mothers for solace. Many similar incidents were characterized by loss of urinary control, shame, and em-barrassment, and then a turning to the mother both for solace and in anger. During our analysis of our data, it gradually became apparent to us that each of these incidents had been preceded by masturbation or by exposure to the sight of male genitals, usually in the course of diapering or toileting of another infant. The sequence consisted of genital self-stimulation or voyeuristic stimulation, leading to sexual arousal; feelings of urinary incompetence and envy inevi-tably followed. Thus, these sequences culminated in the simultaneous discharge of urine and sexual tension, and sexual arousal in these girls became inextricably intertwined with concurrent shame, embarrassment, and anger. The mother was then sought out for comforting to alleviate the feeling of shame. However, since it was precisely the mother whom the girl held responsible for her urinary-genital configuration—one she shared with her mother—conflicting feelings were inevitably aroused. Mutual sexual identification with the mother served to allay the anxiety to some extent, but it also apparently fostered a regression to earlier genital feelings the girl had presumably experienced at the hands of her mother during diapering, bathing, and other times of closeness. Mother and daughter would then become tender and affectionate, an interaction with a definite erotic undertone. I believe that the early mother-daughter relationship is normally characterized by an erotic component, if a true identification is to develop between them. But the erotism has a soothing rather than arousing quality, and does not ordinarily lead to masturbation. Under unusual circumstances, however, this very early mother-daughter sexual erotism may intensify, leading to infantile masturbation during the first year of life, as Greenacre (1952) long ago suggested.

This familiarity with the early pattern in which the affect of shame occurs during the preoedipal period and in the context of genital discovery and arousal has been very helpful in deciding how it can be managed most effectively when it appears within the transference relationship. Anthony (1981) has described some conditions in women where shame seemed to play an inordinate role, although he did not exclude some men of certain types. One such woman had a life history of timidity and exaggerated stranger reaction during the toddler phases, and extreme shyness and timidity during latency. Anthony attributes the major psychopathology to preoedipal causes, principally a marked symbiotic tie to the mother. He believes that normal female development renders the young woman particularly susceptible to pathological "shame syndromes" based upon primary shame. Anthony suggests that this primary shame is connected with early narcissistic injuries at the hands of narcissistically pathological mothers, and advocates working through of these shame feelings early in treatment, to facilitate their transformation, at least in part, into guilt and depression.

In my experience this "working through" process often proves extremely difficult because such feelings as preoedipal shame are experienced largely on a physiological level and have to be translated into psychologically communicative terms. Anthony quotes Schur (1960) in describing shame as tending to be more physiological, with its wide range of autonomic reactions, and nearer the phase of infantile preverbal psychosomatic states, whereas guilt, a somewhat later development, is more psychologically communicative and less archaic in its expression.

When the affects of shame and embarrassment emerged in the fifteen- or sixteen-month-old girls in our research sample, they seemed to immediately contribute to a sense of lowered self-esteem and, inevitably, to an excessive tendency to self-blame at a somewhat later period of life. This early experience of shame and embarrassment is a basic component in the genesis of the psychopathology in many of my adult women patients, interfering substantially with the development of a satisfactory sense of self. Among the many determinants of the sense of self in girls is, of course, the nature of the mother's own sense of self. It would seem likely that the degree to which a mother can allow her preoedipal erotic tie to her daughter to dissolve (instead of retaining it to support her own narcissistic needs) is crucial for the child's further sense of self, particularly her sense of sexual identity. In my patient's case, she had as a small child, been required to fulfill her mother's special need for the mother-female child duality; despite the birth of the patient's brother during the latter part of my patient's second year, it was my patient to whom her mother repeatedly turned. I assume this served to fill the mother's sense of emptiness, the result of her own earlier experiences of having been denied the mother-girl-child erotic closeness with her own mother.

Many recent infancy studies have demonstrated the transmission of affect from mother to infant, even from the earliest months. As Miller (1981) has speculated, this must mean that the secret life of the parents, including their sexuality, unintegrated by the parents themselves and therefore equally unintegrated by their children, is absorbed by the very young infant. Only to the degree that the parents need not use the infant for their own narcissistic purposes, sexual or nonsexual, is the child free to develop along his own innate lines, with neither an excessive need to please the parents nor an excessive degree of frustration of his wishes. The child's own attributes, including sexual attributes, can then be integrated as part of the sense of self. However, as Miller has pointed out, when the parents' narcissism demands considerable sacrifice of the child's spontaneous feelings, a sense of falseness of the self and internal impoverishment may ensue, with a parallel loss of affective aliveness in the emerging capacity for object love, or unmanageable states of sexual as well as aggressive tension. This is the situation that prevailed in my patient, reflected by many indications of her constant struggle to free herself of the intolerable burden of her mother's narcissistic investment.

I think that the sense of emptiness and loneliness so often described by women, and their tendency to experience intense sexual arousal only to be followed by disappointment and shame, are later reflections of early experiences in which the depressed mother attempts to assuage her emptiness and sexual longing through temporary revival of the mother-child tie of her own childhood, including its erotic aspect. While these maneuvers probably do not succeed in ameliorating the maternal depression, they may lead to the mechanism described by Miller in which young infants put aside their own feelings and fantasies, including erotic ones, in favor of attempting to fill the narcissistic requirement of the parent.

This early experience of excessive arousal by the mother, followed by anger and disappointment, is then vigorously suppressed; instead, an unending search for a close erotic relationship with one person after another takes its place. It is then within the transference that the reality of the early experience of the sense of maternal deprivation emerges. Recognition of the impossibility of undoing this early experience is a necessary prerequisite for giving up the endless and fruitless quest, but it is only within the transference itself that this can be initiated, and only then extended to the area of relationships with others. The performance of this therapeutic task requires those qualities in the therapist alluded to by Stone (1981)—the sense of indestructability, dependable patience over time, empathy of course, and flexibility while remaining within the therapeutic framework. This therapeutic work must also effect the patient's gradual disillusionment with the magical belief that the therapist can perform the unattainable righting of the ancient wrong.

My patient had expected that by coming to a woman analyst (she had been in psychotherapy for several years with a male therapist before this), my magical power would fill her emptiness and resolve her feelings of worthlessness in a passive way, without her active participation in the task. This initial hope was followed by a long period of gradual disillusionment marked by quite serious regressions, including somatic symptoms, a sense of complete worthlessness, and feelings of self-dissolution which were often of alarming proportions. The tendency toward marked and sudden regression was coupled, however, with a parallel capacity for equally rapid reconstitution. This pattern of organization is often seen in the young child, and has seemed to me, by and large, to be more marked in women patients. In these women, sudden regressions have been mobilized by such extratherapeutic events as examination reactions (which I have described elsewhere; Galenson, 1983) and the loss of important love objects. These sudden and massive regressions which characterize the transference are mobilized by even short separations from the therapist or changes in scheduling. I believe they reflect the pattern of the pre-oedipal shifts during childhood and infancy from expression through physiological channels to the more advanced level of psychological functioning. This propensity is important in regard to somatic and other archaic reflections in the transference.

The variety of transference manifestations I have alluded to in this panorama of preoedipal reflections share at least one basic feature in that they stem largely from the preverbal period. Stone (1981) describes this particular developmental epoch as a period during which verbal communication has not yet afforded a bridge over separation between mother and child; he points out that only as speech develops does it begin to serve as a vehicle of a different order for the expression of needs, affects, or other psychological states. Then the somatic bond loosens, and with this the power of parental unconscious fantasies begins to wane. However, where these bonds do not loosen, despite speech development, the child searches for relief from unpleasant affects through more regressive forms of gratification, usually oral in nature. In adults who have suffered such childhood experiences, the use of food, pills, alcohol, and smoking reflect attempts to satisfy these regressive needs. Hypochondriasis is also a frequent symptom of an underlying fear of bodily disintegration, and somatization of other types indicates the channelization of psychological disturbance through these pathways of early infancy.

The achievement of separation from the mother, as reflected in the transference attachment and its resolution, can be accomplished eventually, but the leave-taking must of course be initiated by the patient herself. This constitutes the most difficult aspect of transference management. What has been done can never be undone, but substitute relationships with other women, with whom the inner feminine erotic life may be shared, offers a satisfactory partial alternative for many women once the sense of separateness begins to be achieved. Alternatively, a newfound capacity for work or play may emerge once the early role as the mother's alter ego is at least partially abandoned and the patient begins to take on greater responsibility for her own therapeutic advance.

In summary, the preoedipal material reflected in the transference in the woman I described was characterized by homosexual wishes and feelings of shame, archaic transference manifestations which emerged in contemplation of a final separation from the therapist. A genetic and structural connection was suggested between these particular archaic aspects of the transference on the one hand, and infantile experiences, on the other, which had involved sexual arousal, feelings of genital inadequacy, and resulting anger at her mother. This constellation coincides in form, pattern of drive organization, and defensive structure with our own research findings in many girls during the same era of life. The mother's narcissistic use of her young child arouses premature and excessive sexual tension as well as anger, which were discharged in this patient through temper tantrums in her early years. This mixture of erotic and hostile feelings toward the mother, particularly where the mother's unpredictable narcissistic needs cause an unusual type and degree of ambivalence in the child, may provide the genetic groundwork for a definitive form of sadomasochism during the oedipal period. The unusual type of sexual arousal in this instance contrasts with the soothing type of sexuality which ordinarily characterizes the early mother-child relationship, the latter providing the basic ingredient for the development of a sound sense of self, including the sense of early genital sexuality.

The transference relationship in the patient I have described was also characterized by sudden and severe regressive and progressive shifts, often involving resomatization, a pattern which characterizes infantile organization during the first two or so years of life. Such shifts seem to be more common in women than in men and may be due to a greater persistence of the preoedipal tie between mother and daughter.

Familiarity and greater acceptance by the patient of the actuality of the deficiency in early object relations must be accomplished within the transference, in both psychotherapeutic and analytic work. Only then can the patient begin to surrender the repetitive search for replacement of this earlier deficiency in object relationships.

Finally, I would want to emphasize my belief that, although the patient described in this paper happened to be in analytic treatment, these issues could have been raised and dealt with in the same manner within a psychoanalytically oriented psychotherapeutic situation. I agree with Stone's position (1981) that an analytic type of therapy can be conducted in which transference issues emerge and can be worked with in a manner similar to that in analytic treatment.

## REFERENCES

Anthony, E.J. (1981), Shame, guilt, and the feminine self in psychoanalysis. In: *Object and Self: A Developmental Approach: Essays in Honor of Edith*

*Jacobson*, ed. S. Tuttman, C. Kaye, & M. Zimmerman. New York: International Universities Press, pp. 191–234.

Galenson, E. (1983), Infancy research and clinical implications for women. Unpublished manuscript.

——— Roiphe, H. (1976), Some suggested revisions concerning early female development. In: *Female Psychology*, ed. H. Blum (Suppl. *J. Amer. Psychoanal. Assn.*, 24(5):29–57). New York: International Universities Press, 1977.

Greenacre, P. (1952), Some factors producing different types of genital and pregenital organization. In: *Trauma, Growth, and Personality*, New York: Norton.

Miller, A. (1981), *Prisoners of Childhood*. New York: Basic Books.

Roiphe, H., & Galenson, E. (1982), *Infantile Origins of Sexual Identity*. New York: International Universities Press.

Schur, M. (1960), Phylogenesis and ontogenesis of affect and structure-formation and the phenomenon of repetition compulsion. *Internat. J. Psycho-Anal.*, 41:275–287.

Stone, L. (1981), Notes on the non-interpretive elements in the psychoanalytic situation and process. *J. Amer. Psychoanal. Assn.*, 29:89–118.

# 7

# The Interactional Aspect of Transference: Range of Application

## MERTON M. GILL, M.D.

The discussion of the role of transference in a psychoanalytically oriented psychotherapy inevitably implies a perspective on the relationship between psychoanalysis and psychotherapy as modes of treatment. I believe it has been abundantly clear that psychoanalysis and psychotherapy are significantly different treatment modalities and that it is important to emphasize and maintain the distinction. I agree that there is a vital distinction. I make this point at the outset because in earlier presentations of my point of view on transference I have learned that I am often misunderstood and am considered to be arguing against a distinction between psychoanalysis and psychotherapy. What I will argue is quite a different proposition, a proposition which at first glance may seem to narrow the distinction between psychoanalysis and psychotherapy but which in fact makes them even further apart than they are often considered to be. My proposition is that there is a central analytic technique—the analysis of transference—and that this technique is applicable in a much broader range of conditions than is often considered the case. By conditions I refer to frequency of sessions, whether the couch is used, the severity of the disorder, and the experience of the therapist. That is, I believe this central technique—and I mean the analysis of the transference—is applicable even if sessions are held only once or twice a week, the couch is not used, the patient is sicker than is ordinarily considered appropriate for analysis, and the therapist is relatively inexperienced.

The argument rests on a conception of transference somewhat different from the one which leads to the conclusion that it develops, and safely so, only in the usual conditions of analysis. This different conception of transference is what is referred to, in the title of my presentation, as the interactional aspect of transference.

The central intrinsic technical distinction between psychoanalysis and psychotherapy relates to the analysis of the transference. In broadest terms, in psychoanalysis the development of the transference is encouraged and the analysis of the transference is a central if not indeed the primary technique; whereas in psychotherapy the transference is discouraged from developing and plays a role in technique only insofar as it intrudes itself into the therapy despite the therapist's efforts to discourage it.

The role of the analysis of the transference and the conditions of the treatment are in fact two aspects of the same issue, for the conditions considered necessary for the conduct of an analysis are those believed essential for the development and analysis of the transference. Frequent sessions, the couch, a relatively healthy patient, and an analytically trained therapist are thought to be necessary not only to bring about the development of the transference but also to make it possible to do so safely, that is tolerably for the patient without undue anxiety or the acting out of the transference. What my thesis that the analysis of the transference is applicable in a broader range of conditions amounts to, then, is the argument that these optimal conditions are not essential either for the development of the transference or for safely dealing with it.

I turn now to outline what I mean by an interactional aspect of transference. The lineage of this conception may be seen in part in the reference list included here, specifically Racker (1968) from the Kleinian tradition and Langs (1978) and Lipton (1977) from the Freudian. I have also added Sullivan's interpersonal theory of psychiatry (1953) although Sullivan himself did not do much by way of the *analysis* of transference. That defect of interpersonal psychoanalysis has been significantly remedied by some modern Sullivanians, notably Edgar Levenson in his book, *The Fallacy of Understanding*, which appeared in 1972.[1]

In broadest terms, the interactional aspect of transference rests on conceptualizing the therapeutic situation as an interpersonal one, that is, one in which the experience of the situation for both parties is to be understood as a transaction between them. This view is in no way inconsistent with recognizing that both patient and therapist have potential patterns of interpersonal interaction that are intrapsychically structured, but it does say that the manner in which these patterns will be expressed is shaped by the immediate interpersonal interaction. The crucial shift in emphasis from a prevalent view of transference is to ascribe greater importance to the role of the therapist in determining the patient's experience of the relationship, that is, of the transference. In outline form a more detailed statement of the interactional aspect of transference is this:

1. Because the therapy situation is an interpersonal transaction, transference is continuous rather than occasional; that is, transference does not have to be encouraged

---

[1]Dr. Michels' view, as expressed in this volume, is much more like what I am calling an interactional view of transference than I think is generally to be found in the Freudian psychoanalytic literature.

to be present, since it is always present. I defer for a time the question of whether the conditions considered optimal for analysis are necessary to produce a particular kind of transference, namely, a regressive transference, even if it be conceded that transference is ubiquitously present.

2. The patient is in varying degrees inhibited from openly expressing the experience of the interaction, a phenomenon generally referred to as resistance. For this reason this experience is, to a significant degree, expressed in compromise formations—that is, in disguised and indirect allusions rather than in explicit reference. The more one directs one's attention to the allusive references to the transference, the more one becomes convinced that the transference is continuous and not intermittent.

3. With the recognition that the patient's experience of the relationship develops within the transaction, this experience is seen as plausibly emerging from this transaction rather than as an inappropriate distortion of an objectively definable real situation. In other words, the emphasis shifts from looking upon the transference as determined solely by the patient in essential disregard of the current therapeutic situation to understanding how, at the very least, the transference has been stimulated by or is a response to the therapist. I say "at the very least" because the respective contributions of patient and analyst to the patient's experience of the relationship vary in a wide range. At one extreme of this range, the experience is primarily derived from a relatively implausible interpretation of the therapist's behavior, while at the other extreme the therapist's experience is primarily derived from a relatively implausible interpretation of the patient's behavior. The latter conclusion is what is defined by some as countertransference.

In a broad sense this view of an interactional aspect of transference rests upon a particular view of the nature of the reality of an interpersonal transaction. This is that what goes on between two people cannot be objectively and unequivocally characterized but is subject to varying interpretations depending on the point of view of the interpreter; that is, the inherent ambiguity of interpersonal relations is such that patient and therapist may have quite different though equally plausible understandings of their transaction.

I turn now to some of the implications of this interactional aspect of transference for the technique of the analysis of transference:

1. On the assumption of the central importance of making the patient's experience of the relationship explicit and with the recognition of how differently two people can interpret their transaction, it is first of all necessary that the therapist clearly understand what the patient's experience of the relationship in fact is. This may require asking about what is unclear. It must be remembered, and I mention it as an illustration of the principle of transaction, that asking, like any other behavior on the therapist's part, will also play a role in the patient's experience.

2. Because of the ubiquity of transference and its frequent expression in disguise, the therapist will be alert to the allusions to the transference in what the patient says that is not manifestly about the transference. Reference to the therapist by an allusion is of course recognized by all therapists. I am emphasizing its ubiquity. The interpretation of these allusions can be called interpretations of resistance to the *awareness* of transference in contrast to interpretation of resistance to the *resolution* of transference.

It is important that we not mechanically assume that anything the patient says is an allusion to the transference. The therapist should base an interpretation of such an allusion on some specific evidence that makes such an interpretation plausible. This evidence is likely to be either something the patient has said explicitly about his experience of the relationship or something the therapist has said or done which could plausibly account for some inference the patient makes that results in how he or she experiences the relationship.

3. Recognition that the patient's experience derives from the transference means that in principle there is always some contribution by the therapist to the patient's experience. Earlier I described the range of the relative contributions of patient and therapist. Now I emphasize that what is important in the therapy is not the assessment by an external observer but the assessments reached by patient and therapist. All three—patient, therapist, and observer—may reach quite different judgments.

I suggest that no matter how the therapist assesses his or her contribution to the patient's experience it is important to clarify how the patient assesses it and the specific data on which the patient bases his view. It may be difficult to determine what the patient considers this contribution to be, because often the patient is strongly motivated to disavow what he considers the therapist's contribution. It is important to recognize that the reason for this disavowal will frequently be that he thinks the therapist would be made uncomfortable by what the patient believes he has perceived.

4. With the clarification of what the patient views as the therapist's contribution, the patient is now more likely to reassess his evaluation of his experience, that is to say, to assess his own contribution. In other words, this is the beginning of the work of resolution of the transference.

5. It will be apparent that the technique outlined inevitably focuses heavily on the immediate interaction between patient and therapist, what is sometimes called the here and now. Correspondingly, emphasis has shifted away from the there and then, that is, from resolution of the transference by recollection and reconstruction of the past. I believe that the relative roles of present and past in the resolution of transference needs to be reexamined. My prejudice is that

the past has been unduly emphasized. I believe it is often resorted to by both participants as an escape from the discomfort of the present. The importance of the recovery of the past in bringing about resolution of the transference may also vary from case to case. In any event, I believe it is preferable for genetic data to emerge on the patient's initiative rather than the therapist's.

While my sketch of the interactional aspect of transference and its analysis clearly has implications for the conduct of an analysis, my present task is to make more plausible my opinion that with this understanding of transference its analysis can and should be the essential technique, even in conditions other than those considered necessary for analysis. I begin my argument by globally distinguishing between two types of case, the less sick and the more sick, because the reasons offered for restricting the range of application of analysis of the transference differ for these two types. Essentially it is said that unless the usual conditions such as frequency and the use of the couch are met, the transference will not develop in the less sick cases; contrastingly, while it will develop in the more sick, it is dangerous to encourage it.

A crucial issue here is apparently that of regression. It becomes clear that there is a close tie between the concepts of transference and regression. In less sick cases, it is believed, the ordinary conditions of analysis are necessary to bring about a regression that will enable the transference to appear; in more sick, that is, regressed patients, however, the transference will appear even without these conditions, though it cannot be adequately controlled in their absence.

When the interactional aspect of transference I have described is taken into account, these objections lose much of their force. The two kinds of case differ not in the fact that transference is present in the one and not in the other, but rather in how the transference is manifested in each. In the less sick cases the transference is expressed to a more significant degree by allusion. It is not necessary to regress the less sick patient in order for the transference to emerge. What is necessary is to interpret allusions to the transference in what the patient says that is not manifestly about the transference.

Even if one were to concede much of what I have said, it could still be maintained that the kind of transference that is obtainable in less sick patients seen less frequently and in the chair is different from the transference obtained in the usual analytic situation. In general terms it could be said that this transference will be more superficial, more reality-oriented. The so-called deeper, more regressive, more pathological transferences would not develop or at least might be much less readily discernible. This might well be true. Indeed it would be consistent with my view of transference to agree that the conditions of treatment will play a significant role in determining the nature of the transference. My first reply is that I am not arguing that the same thing will happen in the therapy even in differing conditions, but rather that the technique of analysis of the transference that I have described should be employed under varying conditions of therapy. At the same time I am not ready to concede that the difference in the transference under these varying conditions is necessarily so great. Somewhat paradoxically, I will in fact suggest that where this difference seems very great this is perhaps not to the advantage of the therapy. Here I mean to raise the question of whether, with the prevalent conception of transference and with the usual specifications of analysis, an undesirable and unnecessary regression may be produced.

To turn first, however, to the question of the safety of encouraging the transference in more sick patients, here there are several points to be made. First, it is an illusion to imagine that the transference will go away if it is ignored.

It may instead be expressed more overtly in behavior outside the therapy, where its repercussions may be even more dangerous for the patient. Alternatively, it may be driven underground in the therapy situation, where again it is less likely to be subject to control than if it is dealt with explicitly.

Second, if the interactional aspect of transference is taken into account, analysis of the transference may become significantly less threatening to the patient. Instead of dealing with the transference as an inappropriate distortion of the present that reveals how sick the patient is, the therapist will look for something in the present transaction that makes the patient's experience at least understandable from his or her point of view. This attitude toward the transference will make it more likely that what will be dealt with will be ideas present in the patient's awareness that he or she is inhibited from voicing or that are at most preconscious ideas, rather than the therapist's speculations about the patient's unconscious. It is this latter kind of interpretation, correct or not, that is likely to be dangerous.

Third, because the ordinary conditions of analysis are believed to exert pressure toward regression, the analytic technique is considered by many unsuitable for sicker patients. What I have described does not foster regression and therefore seems to me to broaden the spectrum of patients with whom the analytic technique can be used.

Before returning to the view to which I have alluded—that the consequences of inducing regression are unfortunate and unnecessary—I must briefly consider another but closely related idea frequently offered as a reason why analysis of the transference requires the usual conditions for analysis. Only in the presence of such conditions, it is argued, can an uncontaminated transference be revealed. I hope it is by now clear how very illusory the notion of an uncontaminated transference is if the view I have described is correct. However much the blank screen model is disavowed by analysts, I believe it persists in various guises. One of these is the idea of an uncontaminated transference developing from within the patient alone.

In fact, and I can turn now to my criticism of the alleged necessity for regression in the analytic situation, there is a paradoxical inconsistency in the ideas that the transference should be uncontaminated, on the one hand, and that the conditions of analysis should induce regression, on the other. What results if a regression is induced can hardly be considered spontaneous and uncontaminated. More specifically, it can hardly be considered the reproduction of an infantile neurosis. One of the reasons that this inconsistency can escape notice is that it is not realized that the conditions of therapy are part of the therapist's contribution to the transaction and as such provide an aspect of what makes the patient's experience of the relationship understandable. As a gross example I instance the common experience that it feels dangerous or humiliating to lie down in the presence of the unseen and seated analyst. In accordance with the technique I am describing, these conditions of treatment need to be explicitly taken into account as the first step toward resolution of the transference. It is in the pursuit of the uncontaminated regressive transference neurosis that the therapist may be led to the stiff withdrawn attitude so often caricatured. Rather than a spontaneous transference, what is produced by a therapist who behaves in this way is a reaction to that behavior, a reaction also determined, of course, by the patient's intrapsychic structure. It can lead to the sort of iatrogenic, unnecessary, and even harmful regression so clearly criticized by Leo Stone in his monograph (1961) on the analytic situation.

As another example of how the conditions of treatment play a role in the transference, and as an indication that one cannot assume how a particular setting will be experienced by a particular patient, I return to the matter of lying down. Rather than as frightening or humiliating, it may be experienced as being cared for and "held," to use Winnicott's term (1965). The experience must be elucidated in each individual instance.

It is appropriate to say a word about free association here, since many believe that the transference cannot be analyzed unless the patient free associates and that a patient cannot free associate unless the usual conditions of analysis obtain. The idea of free association may carry some of the same incorrect implications as the idea of an uncontaminated transference. Freud (1900) noted that free association is determined by concealed purposive ideas, two major sets of which concern the illness and the therapist (pp. 531–532). He might well have made more explicit the point that the patient's associations are influenced by the therapeutic setting as well as by the therapist's interventions. Every time the analyst intervenes he may be experienced as suggesting a direction for the patient to pursue. All that the rule of free association can mean is that the patient is intermittently given the opportunity to express his thoughts freely and that after intervening the therapist returns to giving the patient free rein and is alert to the consequences of his interventions on the patient's flow of ideas. Freud (1926) referred to analysis as a conversation, not a soliloquy (p. 187).

The conclusion that the analysis of transference as I have described it should be employed in a broader range of conditions raises many questions both about prevalent beliefs and practices as well as about the difficulties, disadvantages, and dangers of a changed practice. I can now only touch on a few of these questions. I should make it explicit that I am not describing a point of view which I can claim to have been adequately tested outside the ordinary conditions for analysis but rather one with which I have done some work and which I consider to be a plausible set of ideas that should be tested over a broad range of therapies and therapists.

One question to be raised is the kind of training and experience required to engage in such work. I make the unorthodox suggestion that it should be taught from the beginning to all who propose to engage in insight-oriented psychotherapy. Obviously the skill with which it will be conducted will depend on the aptitude of the therapist and on his experience. A danger one might seem to be courting here is "wild analysis." This refers, however, to a gross lack of tact in pointing out something to a patient which the therapist thinks he has discerned about him, with no consideration of how he might feel about such knowledge. My experience in teaching this technique has been that such errors are not increased by a beginner's dealing with the here and now of the relationship as best as he is able to understand it. It must also be remembered that an important safeguard lies in abandoning techniques designed to increase regression.

A more serious danger is that the patient may experience the emphasis on the transference as a seduction to intimacy. The therapist may respond to a greater or lesser degree and then become alarmed, either because he feels he is violating what he has been taught is the proper reserved professional attitude, or for more personal reasons. He may then withdraw, leaving the patient bewildered. I am not suggesting that such a sequence is either unusual or unmanageable, but that an inexperienced therapist may be unable to see and deal with it. At the same time I believe there are automatic safeguards, as it were, in interpersonal interaction. Both patient and therapist are likely to be quite tentative before seriously committing themselves. To the extent to which they must withdraw from each other, the analysis of the transference will be cut short. But should we not expect that the inexperienced therapist will accomplish less than the experienced?

Another unorthodox suggestion pertains to the choice of therapy. The present procedure is generally to choose a therapy after a diagnostic study. That choice can often be globally characterized as for or against making the analysis of the transference the primary therapeutic technique. If the range of applicability of the analysis of transference is considered to be increased, it becomes reasonable to attempt to apply it across the board. I believe this can be done and that it can be done with the flexibility required by different kinds of pathology but without abandoning the principle of making the analysis of the transference primary. In my experience such practice not uncommonly heightens the goal of what a patient wants from therapy. But should we be the ones to limit goals in advance? The choice of therapy and the setting of goals, like the conditions of therapy, have important repercussions on the patient's experience of the relationship, repercussions that are often not taken into account in understanding that experience. We are all familiar for example, with how some patients react to the advice that they undergo psychotherapy, not psychoanalysis. My suggestion is simply to get down to work without any prior setting of goals.

In summary: I have described the interactional aspect of transference and have suggested that with this broadened view of transference its analysis can and should be used in a much broader range of situations than is ordinarily considered appropriate for a therapy which makes the analysis of transference its central technique. This broadened view of transference and its analysis stresses the following points: transference is continuous and not occasional; its continuous nature becomes more apparent when it is recognized that it is often manifested by allusion rather than explicitly; it arises in an interpersonal transaction and is therefore always understandable and often even plausible in the light of this transaction; the analysis of transference should begin by searching for the therapist's contribution to the transaction; this contribution lies in the conditions of therapy as well as in the therapist's interventions within these conditions.

Finally, I point out that the view of transference that I have described is neutral with regard to differing opinions regarding psychodynamics. I have noted with interest that the same differences of opinion regarding the relation between psychoanalysis and psychotherapy that have long been described in our literature are beginning to appear in discussions of the applicability of what is called self psychology (London, 1980; Palaci, 1980). The crucial feature of the point of view I have presented—which would remain unchanged regardless of the psychodynamic theory espoused—is that the therapeutic relationship is a transaction, not a projection onto a blank screen.

Among many analysts, an almost inevitable reaction to this presentation of the interactional aspect of transference will be that I am abandoning the heart of the analytic understanding of transference, that is, the "intrapsychic" view. As one reviewer of this paper put it, I am throwing out the baby with the bathwater. Emphasis on a different point of view inevitably risks obscuring the more customary one. Transference is a joint product of the patient's intrapsychically structured patterns of relationship and of the interaction with the analyst. The proportions of the contributions from these two sources vary widely from one patient-analyst pair to another, and from one situation to another in any analysis.

It may also be questioned whether the view of transference described here is relevant to psychotherapy. My position is that analysis of the transference can be made the primary technique in a broader range of circumstances—with regard to frequency, recumbency, pathology of patient, experience of therapist—than is usually considered possible. If one insists on referring to therapy in this extension as psychotherapy, then I am describing the analysis of transference in psychotherapy. But I believe it very misleading to use the term psychotherapy here, as it ordinarily refers to a therapy in which the transference is sometimes manipulated and is analyzed only more or less, occasionally rather than consistently. I prefer to think of the therapy I am describing as the employment of psychoanalytic technique in a broad range of circumstances.[1]

## References

Freud, S. (1900), The Interpretation of Dreams. *Standard Edition*, 4–5. London: Hogarth Press, 1953.

——— (1926), The question of lay analysis. *Standard Edition*, 20:183–250. London: Hogarth Press, 1959.

Gill, M. (1982), *Analysis of Transference Volume I: Theory and Technique*. New York: International Universities Press.

——— (1984), Psychoanalysis and psychotherapy: A revision. *Internat. Rev. Psycho-Anal.*, 11:161–179.

——— (1984–85), The range of applicability of psychoanalytic technique. *Internat. J. Psychoanal. Psychother.*, 10:109–116

Langs, R. (1978), *Technique in Transition*. New York: Jason Aronson.

Levenson, E. (1972), *The Fallacy of Understanding*. New York: Basic Books.

Lipton, S. (1977), The advantages of Freud's technique as shown in his analysis of the Rat Man. *Internat. J. Psycho-Anal.*, 58:255–274.

London, N. (1980), Discussion of "Psychoanalysis of the self and psychotherapy" by Jacques Palaci. In: *Advances in Self Psychology*, ed. A. Goldberg. New York: International Universities Press, pp. 337–347.

Palaci, J. (1980), Psychoanalysis of the self and psychotherapy. In: *Advances in Self Psychology*, ed. A. Goldberg. New York: International Universities Press, pp. 317–335.

Racker, H. (1968), *Transference and Countertransference*. New York: International Universities Press.

Stone, L. (1961), *The Psychoanalytic Situation*. New York: International Universities Press.

[1]The reader may be interested in two other writings of mine on the same theme as this chapter. (See Gill, 1984 and 1984–85).

Sullivan, H. (1953), *The Interpersonal Theory of Psychiatry*. New York: Norton.

Winnicott, D. (1965), *Maturational Process and the Facilitating Environment*. New York: International Universities Press.

# 8

# Interpretation and Psychoanalytic Psychotherapy: A Clinical Illustration

## JACOB A. ARLOW, M.D.

Since theory divorced from clinical material can be viewed in many different ways, it was suggested to me that the report of an actual experience in therapy would be useful in illustrating the principles we have been discussing. At the same time, such material might serve as a point of departure in considering the relative merits of the various approaches that have been offered. Accordingly, I will describe material from the first two sessions with a patient. I will then proceed to explain the principles underlying the conceptualization of the case and the approach to understanding and interpreting the transference. These principles—dynamics, conflict, and compromise formation—apply to mental functioning in general, as well as to the process of pathogenesis and to therapy.

The patient was a young unmarried woman who was referred to me recently when her doctor became physically incapacitated. She had been seeing him twice a week for somewhat over four years. The patient had had my name for several weeks before she called me. When she did call, she said she was going out of town and would call again on her return. She called me ten days later and it seemed very difficult to arrange a time, but finally a mutually acceptable date was agreed upon.

On the day of the appointment she arrived fifteen minutes late. She had forgotten to get off the bus at the proper corner. The patient was a woman in her mid-twenties, well spoken, fairly attractive, alert, vivacious, and ingratiating. Talking to her revealed that she was obviously of very superior intelligence. Some difficulties, however, began to appear almost immediately. Ordinarily I begin by asking a few questions in order to place the patient in the objective world. I inquire about age, occupation, marital status, education, family, any serious illnesses, and any history of previous psychotherapy. This time I did not get very far. The patient spoke clearly, but in obsessive detail, about nonessentials. It was difficult to budge her from the direction she chose to follow. Finally I decided to relinquish the lead entirely to her. First she spoke about feeling depressed and about her difficulty in getting on with men. She kept referring to two men she had been seeing, switching quickly and quietly from one to another without identifying them in any specific way. Finally I asked her if she could identify each one at least by his first name, so I could keep the two of them separate in my mind.

On her own she turned to give me some information about her family. Her father is a self-made man who overcame great hardships. In her early upbringing, women were considered of no account, and her education was sexually segregated. Her academic career, which was extensive, indicated clearly that she must have been a brilliant student, although she does not think so. She could have been accepted at the same professional school her younger brother now attended, but for various reasons chose not to apply. From this, she turned to a meticulously detailed and elaborately recited account of the onset of her menses. This subject took up almost the entire remainder of the interview. It was indeed a most distressing story. There were serious endocrinological, metabolic, dermatological, arthritic, and other difficulties, and these had been variously diagnosed by different doctors. The patient tried to decide which of the two leading specialists in the field she should follow. One thought the condition to be very serious; the other felt it was self-limiting and would soon disappear. It was hard to ascertain which of the doctors she really believed; in the end it seems she accepted one man's diagnosis but followed the other man's treatment.

My own reaction to her recital at this point was interesting. On the one hand I felt deeply moved by the overwhelming suffering that so young a girl had to experience at such a crucial period in her life; on the other, however, I detected a certain challenging bitterness in her recital to me. The total effect upon me was "What a welcome to womanhood!"

The patient was unswerving in her determination to give the details of the treatment. How the referrals were made and the account of the laboratory tests, most of which were well beyond my knowledge, what opinions were reached, and the paths by which the doctors arrived at their conclusions were all laid out in great detail. It was, in fact, difficult to follow the case history as it unfolded or to keep relevant facts in mind, since the patient did not make any effort to supply the data in a summarizing, orderly fashion. After a while, it was clear that she was going to tell the story her way and I was just going to have to listen. Every once in a while, thoughts of conflict with her brother intruded into her discussion, although the patient feels that she has no problem in this area whatsoever. Nonetheless, ideas of competition and retaliation kept recurring.

At the end of the session I told her that I thought it would be important to know something of what happened in her treatment with her previous therapist, what she had learned about her problems from him. She replied by describing at great length what a wonderful physician she thought he was, but she could not give any of the details of the treatment at the time or what she had learned. However, she did make reference to a number of other doctors she had consulted before and after her previous therapist, for purposes of engaging in psychotherapy. All of these comments were disparaging. At the end of the session, I told her that at the next meeting it would be useful if we could begin by discussing what she had gotten from her treatment with Dr. X.

We then set about establishing the date for the next meeting. Here the patient claimed there was some difficulty, but she did not make clear just what the difficulty was. She did say, however, that she would let me know if the time that I suggested to her was acceptable, but she could not say so at the present time. Later in the week she waited until the last minute to call to confirm the time of the appointment. It turned out that there had really been no practical conflict at all.

The next consultation was held a week later. This time the patient was sixteen minutes late. She had walked right past the door of my building and had kept on going for about seven or eight minutes before she realized her mistake. When I asked if she had some problem with lateness, she said, "Sometimes."

Then I asked her if she remembered my suggestion at the end of the last session about how we should begin this one. She looked entirely blank. She had no recollection that I had made any such statement. She certainly did not recall the subject that I had proposed we talk about. I reminded her that I was interested in finding out what happened in her treatment with Dr. X. She made some vague sign of recognition and then proceeded to give a detailed account of her relationship with her boyfriend, A, with no mention whatsoever of the question I had put to her. She stopped after about ten minutes and said, "You know, I am not telling you what you asked me about." Thus she made sure that I knew what she was doing. I told her to proceed in whatever way she felt was best for her.

The story that she gave of her love life was meticulously described insofar as insignificant details were concerned. Her boyfriend, A., is a brilliant, successful, but neurotic young man. They have had a five-year relationship. After three years, he had proposed marriage, but the very next morning had called up and said that he had seen his therapist, who suggested he might be rushing things. Fortunately, the patient said, she had not told anyone about the proposal she had received the night before. A. had thought things over and wanted to delay making a decision. A short time later, however, he proposed again but this time she rejected him. Since that time, she explained, he has proposed and she has proposed; the relationship has been on and off, on and off, on and off. They never can get together on a decision at the same time. Listening to her account, I had the thought, "This is a kind of cat-and-mouse game."

In the interim she has seen a number of other men and followed a similar pattern with them. She gets involved with them and at a certain point receives a proposal of marriage. At such times she is beset with doubt, and soon afterward finds some reason to precipitate a breakup. Each time she has found that she is really interested in her original boyfriend, A. She cannot give him up and through all the other relationships would go back to see him from time to time. At one point A. received an offer from a prestigious professional firm from out of town. It was a job that he had wanted. When it was offered to him, he accepted it immediately by phone. A. then informed my patient that he had accepted the job and now they could get married and go off together to the other city. The patient became furious. How could he have accepted the offer without consulting her? Her anger arose despite the fact that she had been encouraging him to take the position if it was offered. She explained that, considering he had accepted a position without consulting her, she could only anticipate a life where she would be denigrated, disregarded, and not consulted on any of the important decisions.

At that point I observed, "Then you felt that this was a good time to break off the relationship?" "Oh, on the contrary," she replied. She then reported that she has kept on seeing him. This was more than two years ago. He is now in the other city, but she still goes there from time to time to see him. No other man has the same appeal for her as A. She does not know why; she had raised the question with her previous therapist. Then she said to me, "I think I'm so attached to him because he was the first man that I had sexual relations with. Do you think this could have anything to do with it?"

I want to point out three reactions that I had while the patient was talking. First, I was aware of becoming annoyed. I amused myself by thinking that, in my younger days, when I was possessed of greater therapeutic zeal and enthusiasm, I would have tried to pursue various details in which I was interested. This time I just permitted the patient to continue talking. In addition, I noted my ironic reaction, my thought, "Welcome to womanhood," and the metaphor that came to my mind to describe the way in which she interacted with the various men in her life, namely, a cat-and-mouse game.

Now let us examine the principles we use in understanding and planning the treatment of the patient. I said earlier that we would look at the material from the point of view of dynamics, conflict, and compromise formation. First, concerning dynamics: this has to do with the driving force of the unconscious wish. Concepts of what constitutes the nature of the driving forces of the mind have changed in the course of time. Current theory pays greatest attention to derivatives of sexual and aggressive drives. Although theories concerning the origin and nature of the drives may have changed, one principle remains constant, namely, that a major component of both the neurotic process and of normal mental functioning derives from the persistent conscious and unconscious demands stemming from the drives. At a particular point in the developmental history of the individual, certain wishes of childhood become fixed and structuralized. By this I mean that they continue to exert upon the mind a persistent demand for gratification or for actualization. While there are differences of opinion concerning the particular point in the development of the individual at which these dynamic wishes become fixed, there is no question but that such wishes continue to exert a demanding, imperative influence on the mind for their realization.

These unconscious wishes, often translated as fantasy formations, create a mental set, on the basis of which the data of experience are selectively perceived. This is true both in the neurotic process and in the normal way of thinking. In the neurotic process the data of perception are misperceived, misinterpreted, and mistakenly responded to in terms of these persistent unconscious fantasies. The greater the intrusion or the influence of these fantasies, the more severe the pathology; there is a reciprocal interplay between the data of experience, the interactions with individuals, and the unconscious fantasy. The unconscious fantasy gives the mental set around which these data are perceived. The perceptions, on the other hand, tend to arouse selectively certain of the unconscious wishes; they are reminders and stimulators of what is latent and persistent.

The principles behind the organization of treatment reflect the dynamic imperative of the instinctual drives. In the setting of the kind of treatment that permits patients to say whatever they wish, the physician is in a position to study the record of the variations and the vicissitudes of the derivative manifestations of the basic wishful fantasies. The therapist can observe not only the events that take place within the treatment situation, but also attitudes and behavior of the patient that relate to the therapist. The therapist is at one and the same time a participant as well as an observer. It is a striking phenomenon, going back to the "Studies on Hysteria" (1895), long before Freud discovered and understood transference,[1] that people tend to repeat certain patterns of relationships and events in their lives. It is this tendency that conveys a sense of coherence to each individual's life history, and that becomes the hallmark of credibility in the works of the truly intuitive novelist or poet. From every patient we soon learn that, while the scenes and the characters change frequently, the plot and the story line of their lives basically remain the same. Sooner or later the therapist is cast in a role as one of the principals in this repetitive drama. This is what constitutes the transference.

In the transference, the patient attempts to foist a role upon the therapist. This is true of practically all forms of psychotherapy. The analytic situation does not create the transference. Transference is not a set of special regressive phenomena induced by being a patient, by lying down, by having someone give undivided attention, or by baring one's secrets in an unbalanced, unequal situation. This is a view that Charles Brenner and I have presented and discussed as far back as the first Pan-American International Psychoanalytic Congress (Arlow and Brenner, 1966). What the patient sees in the particular transaction depends upon the

---

[1]It should be noted that Freud did make reference in this work to the concept of transference (p. 303), but in a more narrow sense than in later writings.

patient, and it varies with each individual, depending upon his or her own experience. Any one or all of the factors just mentioned may be significant, provided they have some resonance with the patient's basic unconscious fantasy and reflect some specific, not general, aspect of the patient's personal history. What is revived in the transference is that which is persistently active as a dynamic force in the patient's mind.

What we reconstruct with any degree of certainty in treatment are the vicissitudes of the patient's struggle with his conflictual wishes—in other words, the transformations of his conflict during the course of his lifetime. Freud alluded to this problem in his paper "Constructions in Analysis" (1937), when he stated that it is improbable, or perhaps impossible, to reactivate latent conflicts. Nunberg (1925) brought the principles of the neurotic process in precise juxtaposition with those of the treatment process when he wrote "The Will to Recovery." There he pointed out that the patient comes to treatment to be relieved of the effects of his conflicts over certain forbidden instinctual wishes; yet, even as he does so, he is unconsciously impelled, that is, driven, to enlist the participation of the therapist in an unconscious attempt to actualize the fantasy, to fulfill the very wishes that initiated the conflict from which he is suffering. In the light of these considerations, the distinction between relations outside the treatment and within it may not be as significant as we have been led to believe. The conditions of the treatment situation permit the neurotic conflicts to appear in clear focus and with much greater intensity. This is because the derivative expressions of the unconscious fantasies emerge undiluted by distracting, interpersonal relations and relatively undistorted by realistic interactions. The data of the treatment process are endogenously determined as far as we are able to control it. The vicissitudes of real-life experience are exogenously influenced. It is not that the neurotic process is inoperative in day-to-day activities. On the contrary, the interplay between realistic perceptions and experience, on the one hand, and persistent unconscious fantasy, on the other, is a constant one (Arlow, 1969). However, outside the treatment it is very difficult to determine in a definitive way to what extent the neurotic process intrudes upon realistic activity and the nature and the meaning of that intrusion. Strict adherence to the principles of the treatment situation enable the process to unfold in such a way that the patient comes to realize, or should come to realize, that his problem is an intrapsychic one, not an interpersonal one.

The second major characteristic of the neurotic process that is carried over into the treatment is what Freud referred to originally as an interplay of forces, that is, mental conflict. As he devised it, the psychoanalytic situation became the setting par excellence for observing the interplay of forces in the mind. Essentially, the psychoanalytic process is a day-to-day, moment-to-moment record of that interaction. The same holds true in spirit, although perhaps to a lesser extent, of the therapeutic process in psychoanalytic psychotherapy. What the treatment situation does is make it possible for the therapist to observe how the dynamic equilibrium in the mind shifts and changes under the influence of current experience, of the transference, and above all, under the influence of the therapist's (or analyst's) interventions and interpretations. And everything the analyst does, even if it is not intended as an interpretation, becomes a dynamic stimulus affecting the equilibrium in the patient's mind. If the analyst moves in his chair or coughs, if he has a gurgle in his stomach he cannot control—all of these have some influence on the interplay of forces.

Essentially, what the therapist does is study the derivatives of the unconscious conflict of forces taking place in the patient's mind. The presenting symptoms of the patient constitute the surface representation of a relatively unstable dynamic equilibrium that he has managed to effect. It is not a satisfactory solution to his problem. The therapist's contribution to the treatment process is to intervene in such a way as to shift the dynamic equilibrium in favor of one or another of the forces in conflict. The patient attempts to reestablish the equilibrium and his attempts to do that give us an opportunity to see how the pathogenic process developed in the first place. The efforts of the therapist are destabilizing of any attempt to reestablish the equilibrium in the course of treatment. Lewin (1955) used the metaphor of dream psychology to dramatize this principle. Psychoanalytic technique, he reminded us, derived originally from an artificially induced form of sleep. What the sleeper does is dream. The dream protects his sleep as long as its contents, latent or manifest, do not arouse anxiety. If they do and the sleeper becomes too anxious, he breaks off the dream and wakes up. By way of analogy, Lewin said, the same process may be observed during treatment. The patient associating freely may be compared with a sleeper dreaming contentedly. If he continues in this spirit, having successfully fended off potentially disturbing thoughts or impulses, the therapist intervenes to offer interpretation of content, which has the effect of arousing the dreamer, as if to say, "Don't you think you should pay attention to this or that element?" On the other hand, if the patient is in a state of strong resistance, he may be compared to a wakeful sleeper, wary of surrendering his control and laying himself open to the danger of potential nightmares. Here the therapist intervenes on the side of defense, in effect reassuring the sleeping patient, as if to say, "Don't be so wakeful. The thoughts that come to you are not real and you don't have to be afraid of them. They are only fantasies."

The third principle by which we judge the data we get is typical of the neurotic process and it finds its counterpart in the treatment process and in life in general. This principle is compromise formation. It corresponds in treatment to what is known as derivatives of the unconscious conflict or fantasy. As a result of the interplay of forces, as Freud said, the repressed material itself will never occur to the patient, but only something which approximates it in an allusive way. The greater the resistance, the more remote will be the substitutive association the patient has to report. There is a certain advantage that accrues to both patient and therapist in this situation. In the psychoanalytic situation, external distractions and interferences have been minimized as much as possible and the material that appears in consciousness is predominantly endogenous in origin. The flow of the inner dialogue or conversation tends to be more continuous and more coherent. The characteristic feature of the patient in the grip of this process is the persistent manner in which the unconscious conflicts subtly but inevitably govern the nature of the material brought into consciousness.

In the clinical material I presented, one can see the persistent way in which the patient brought up the element of competition, injury, having been hurt, being dissatisfied, on the one hand, and, on the other, that of being contrary, frustrating, and ungiving. One must never lose sight of the persistence of the underlying wishes and how they bring derivatives into consciousness. Since they are compromise formations the derivative expressions of the unconscious conflict or fantasies both reveal and conceal the source and the nature of their provenance. As in any conversation—and I refer here to the conversation between the different forces of the mind, an inner discussion that goes on between the different elements contributing to a conflict—the precision of comprehension depends on the sequence and the contiguity of the ideas presented. This makes it possible to understand the flow of thoughts even when one or another element may have been omitted or not heard in the course of the conversation.

Since the communications, verbal and nonverbal, that appear in the course of treatment are in the nature of approximations and allusions to what is really meant, psychic derivatives partake of the nature of metaphor (Arlow, 1979) and must be appreciated as such. The productions of the patient in the psychoanalytic situation, like the metaphoric expressions of the poet, mean more than, and are different from, the precise sense of the words articulated.

To divine what Loewenstein (1957) called the "second" or hidden message in the patient's verbalization, one must appreciate both the context of the data and the implicit, deterministic causal principle that operates when elements appear in sequence and in contiguity. Any particular mental product—a thought, a parapraxis, a dream, a fantasy—taken out of context and not examined as part of the dynamic flow of thoughts in the treatment situation may be interpreted in many different ways, or may even be entirely uninterpretable. Only when seen in the context of their dynamic configuration do such elements really become comprehensible, and all the familiar figures of speech and the elements of repetition of theme, similarity of theme, representation by opposites, and convergence into a coherent configuration facilitate the task of interpretation. In other words, there are objective criteria that we have to apply to the data to make an interpretation. Intuition gives us a quick guide, but cognitive discipline, using specific criteria, confirms the interpretation.

What the analyst or therapist interprets is not just the nature or content of the unconscious wish or fantasy. What he or she really does is explicate the nature of the interaction, explaining the causal links that exist among the various components that are at odds within the patient's mind, as they appear in context. For this reason it is more important to observe how the patient responds to a particular intervention on the part of the therapist than to check on the accuracy of the details of the interpretation. In the course of the evolution of the therapeutic process, how the patient responds to the interventions mirrors or replicates the forms of defense instituted by the ego in the process of pathogenesis. The therapist is able to observe, from the sequential flow of the elements in the patient's productions, how certain aspects of the patient's neurosis came into being. If one renders due attention to how the flow of the material is governed and to its sequential arrangement, as determined by the principle of forces in conflict tending toward compromise formation, errors in technique may be avoided and the progress of therapy enhanced.

Let us turn now to the clinical example and summarize the points to be made. First of all, the transference began without my having done anything except answer the telephone. The transference was a carry-over from the previous doctor. It included a lot of disparaging remarks about other doctors, psychiatrists and nonpsychiatrists alike. The business of playing one doctor against another, one boyfriend against another, contrariness, certain oppositional uncooperativeness, which came out so clearly in the relationship with me, was recapitulated by the patient on her own in the very first interview.

The interpretations were suggested to me in an intuitive way by the three things that I have pointed out: an awareness of a sense of annoyance; my ironic thought, "Welcome to womanhood," as if to say "What a sad introduction to womanhood"; and, finally, the idea of the cat-and-mouse game—that someone was going to be eaten, someone was going to be destroyed. These thoughts that came to my mind represented the product of my intuition, namely, the elaboration of the data into meaningful configurations outside the scope of consciousness. To transform these intuitive thoughts into precise interpretations required a cognitive process, namely, observing how certain ideas were repeated and how a similar theme ran through them, recognizing the contiguity and sequence in which the ideas appeared in the patient's mind and finally how they converged into two or three major ideas suggesting hostility toward physicians who had hurt her and upon whom she wished to take vengeance. In her fantasy, she wished to avenge herself in kind. Since she experienced defloration as a castration, she wanted to do the same to men, especially A.

In this instance our understanding could be carried much further because fortunately Freud had already described patients of this type. In a paper entitled "The Taboo of Virginity" (1918), a paper I highly recommend for further elaboration of this material, Freud noted that certain women remain emotionally bound to the first man with whom they have intercourse. The bond, however, is not one of affection, but of hostility. The woman cannot give up the tie to the man who deflowered her because she has not yet exacted the full measure of the vengeance she wishes to wreak upon him. Knowledge of this sort enables us to plan the course of treatment, the hierarchy of interpretations to be given, in a rational manner. The patient must first be made aware of the hostility implicit in her behavior, of her sense of having been injured in an anatomical way, of the special role that the man who deflowered her played in this pattern of reactions, and of the unconscious fantasy of having been castrated during defloration and of exacting vengeance. Ultimately, at each one of these phases some opportunity will arise to demonstrate to the patient how her interaction with the analyst is influenced by these ideas. This is what constitutes the interpretation of the transference. The essential principle of the entire psychotherapeutic approach, however, is to demonstrate to the patient the persistent effect of the unconscious wishes that originated during childhood, but that continue to intrude upon her current, adult mental life and behavior.

There are many problems of interpreting and managing the transference that appear in psychoanalytic psychotherapy that do not arise in the course of classical psychoanalytic technique. In either setting, transference will develop. The number of times a patient is seen a week is not the decisive factor in the evolution of the transference. The relative infrequency of sessions, however, permits a greater intrusion of current reality into the clinical data, so that it becomes difficult for the therapist to perceive and for the patient to pursue the continuity of the themes in the material. Under such circumstances, much of the transference may remain unanalyzed and when this persists over a period of time, it inevitably results in the patient acting out the impulses or defenses contained in the unconscious fantasy. Because of the infrequency of sessions, it is much more difficult to interpret this kind of acting out in psychoanalytic psychotherapy than in classical psychoanalysis. While face-to-face confrontation really does not interfere with the evolution of the transference, it does tend to influence the therapist to intervene more frequently than might occur under other circumstances.

The psychotherapeutic situation in general tends to be more flexible, less rigidly adhered to than the analytic situation, and the variety of things that go on in the psychotherapeutic setting are hardly as standardized as the analytic setting, which means that it is very hard to make comparisons and specific statements. It behooves the therapist, under such conditions, to be more circumspect in what he says and does and to be more conscious of himself as a participant-observer in the therapeutic interaction.

In many respects, psychoanalytic psychotherapy is more difficult than classical analysis, yet it is becoming increasingly the treatment of choice in preference to analysis. In large measure this is determined by the fact that the choice of therapy nowadays is not always determined by the therapist; more often it is the patient himself who determines what treatment he will receive, and sometimes the choice is made by a third-party payer. Economic realities have changed the balance of forces in psychotherapy and this has, in many subtle ways, influenced the course of technique itself.

In conclusion, I would like to say that with our present state of knowledge it is very difficult, if not impossible, to make a general statement about the specific management of transference and interpretation in psychoanalytic psychotherapy in general. The range of patients and the variety of experience are so broad that one can only comment on principles to be employed. One cannot really formulate a blueprint approach to any particular nosological entity.

## REFERENCES

Arlow, J.A. (1969), Fantasy, memory and reality testing. *Psychoanal. Quart.*, 38:28–51.
———— (1979), Metaphor and the psychoanalytic situation. *Psychoanal. Quart.*, 48:363–385.
———— Brenner, C. (1966), The psychoanalytic situation. In: *Psychoanalysis in the Americas: Original Contributions from the First Pan-American Congress for Psychoanalysis*, ed. R.E. Litman. New York: International Universities Press, pp. 23–43.
Breuer, J. & Freud, S. (1895), Studies on hysteria. *Standard Edition*, 2. London: Hogarth Press, 1956.
Freud, S. (1918), The taboo of virginity (contributions to the psychology of love III). *Standard Edition*, 11:193–208. London: Hogarth Press, 1957.
———— (1937), Constructions in analysis. *Standard Edition*, 23:257–269. London: Hogarth Press, 1964.
Lewin, B.D. (1955), Dream psychology in the analytic situation. *Psychoanal. Quart.*, 24:169–199.
Loewenstein, R.M. (1957), Some thoughts on interpretation in the theory and practice of psychoanalysis. *Psychoanalytic Study of the Child*, 12:127–150. New York: International Universities Press.
Nunberg, H. (1925), The will to recovery. In: *Practice and Theory of Psycho-*

*analysis*. New York: Nervous and Mental Disease Publishing Company, 1948, pp. 75–88.

# 9

# Discussion

Question 1: *Each contributor spoke of the management of the transference but left out specific examples—like, what do you do or say? For example, when Dr. Galenson's patient reported warm feelings toward her, what exactly did she respond? How did she interpret it to the patient?*

*Galenson*: The material reported took place in quite natural sequence in relation to the earlier expressed feelings about her mother. As the patient spoke of how difficult it was to tell me about her feelings toward me, and how shameful and embarrassing it was, I believe the only response I gave at that moment was of assent; that is, it is indeed difficult to talk about such feelings. This is very often simply enough to allow the patient to continue, as it was in this case.

I might comment that with other patients I have at times suspected that they were experiencing erotic feelings toward me which they could not put into words. That is a much more difficult situation to know how to handle, and the response has to differ, as Dr. Arlow has noted, in accord with the need of the individual patient. I do try as much as possible to do with my adult patients what I do with non-verbal children; that is, when they are showing evidences of body reactions that seem to betray erotic feelings, such as blushing, apparent shyness, or looking away, I will simply put into words that they look uncomfortable and that perhaps there are some feelings at the moment of which they don't feel free to speak, but the time may come when they will. I certainly do not insist at that moment, nor in any way say to the patient, "We agreed that you were going to tell me everything that was on your mind."

*Arlow*: The question was once asked of Dr. Nunberg, "What would you say in this situation?"—one which was then outlined to him. Dr. Nunberg replied, "How do I know what I would say? If I were *there*, I would know what to do." The point is that in context, in the continuity of the developing relationship and the development of the material, you know what to say. It is very hard to discuss what to say out of context.

Question 2: *Dr. Arlow, do you think that your interview technique affected somehow what emerged in the first two interviews?*

*Arlow*: My answer to that question is "No, I don't think so." The next question would be "Can you prove it?" I'd say, "No, I can't prove it."

*Gill*: I just want to say that it seems to me obvious that Dr. Arlow did influence what came out in those two interviews, and I don't think it would be very difficult to prove it, insofar as one would simply pay attention to the material. I'm sure that he is aware of this, but I think the way in which he's handling the question has to do with a significant difference in point of view between the two of us, which I hope will become clear as we continue.

Let us look at the very beginning: the patient and Dr. Arlow had trouble reaching an appointment time. Wasn't that already the cat-and-mouse game? And wasn't it true that the manner in which he dealt with that meant that he was playing a cat-and-mouse game with her, and in that sense was he not influencing the kinds of data that emerged in the sessions? Would it not have been very different had he behaved in a way which would have made her understand that she was playing out this cat-and-mouse game with him from the very beginning? Had he done something of that sort, would that not have significantly changed the nature of the interaction? It seems to me that it obviously would have. I believe that that's the essential difference of opinion with regard to the argument about the role that the analyst's behavior plays in developing the analysis, and the importance of making an early interpretation of transference.

In my opinion, if one genuinely accepts the idea that in an analysis (I use the concept of analytic technique rather broadly, as I am sure has been apparent) one attempts to avoid manipulating the transference, one does so in favor of interpreting the transference. I believe that the kinds of things that Dr. Arlow did amounted to playing into the transference. I think that Dr. Arlow is essentially of the opinion that he didn't influence the nature of the patient's productions because he didn't *do* anything. He said he just let it come. I don't think he just let it come. I mean, he did, of course; but what I mean is that his just letting it come is *doing* something. Further, he said that when he was younger, he would have done something different. What would he have done different? He would have pursued her to find out the details. Those are not the only two possibilities—either to pursue her or to just let it come. To pursue her to find out the details, I would agree with him, would be problematic. I imagine he would say, as would I, that that would be a manipulation of the transference. But I think that his failure to do something and his positively doing something—as, for example, in the negotiations about the session—did indeed influence her productions. If, then, there is a third alternative, it is the *interpretation* of the transference.

*Arlow*: I was willing to say that I don't know. Dr. Gill, you don't know either. That is the sad thing about psychotherapy; you don't go over the same ground again. You observe a dynamic interaction, and there are many different ways in which you can intervene at different times. You're not always free to intervene in the way you want. If a patient (as in the case I reported) says, ''Oh, I can't see you Monday at eleven o'clock,'' you have to offer her a different time. It may be part of her game, but you have no choice. You can say yes, you can say no. You can say, ''You're trying to manipulate me,'' you can say, ''You've done this with everybody else and now you're doing it to me.'' But you don't know whether or not she would have told you about the boyfriend from this particular way or not. She may have; she may not have. You just can't prove it!

*Schwaber*: One of the issues that arises from this discussion is whether a sharpened focus on the patient's experience of the therapist's interventions will shed more light on the question raised here—namely, what is the influence of any particular intervention made in the initial hours on the patient's response and, in turn, on the specific direction of the ensuing material? This question can then be extended to address the more general issue of the impact of such a perspective—one that highlights a focus on the *patient's experience* of the therapist's interventions, silent or stated—on our understanding of transference.

Question 3: *Dr. Gill, in your technique, how do you deal with material arising from the past—that is, material that appears significant in developing the patient's interaction patterns?*

*Schwaber*: In responding to that question, Dr. Gill, would you address your definition of transference? Do you, for example, in speaking of the here-and-now interaction in elucidating how the patient experiences the therapist, define *this* as transference? If so, how do you utilize the past in terms of the patient's experience of the immediate relationship and how does your view on this matter bear upon your understanding of transference?

*Gill*: These are not very easy questions to answer. I think that the issue of the role of the past and how one utilizes it is one of the things that I'm least clear about. Nevertheless, there are some things that I think that I can say about it. First of all, it is true that my prejudice, as I think I have indicated, is that the material from the past is very often defensive in the relationship. Either the patient brings it up or the therapist brings it up; or, if the patient brings it up, the therapist pursues it because there is something going on in the immediate interaction about which they are both uncomfortable, from which they want to stay away. Therefore, my first attitude toward it is that I want to be sure that it is not defensive. On the other hand, I also recognize that if one constantly deals with material from the past *that* way, that has *its* repercussions on the relationship too. In my zeal in using this kind of technique, I have often had the experience that the patient comes to the opinion that I don't want to hear anything about the past and therefore will tell me only about the present because he or she wishes to please me, whereupon *that* becomes the issue that has to be dealt with in the transference in the here and now.

As far as the overall question of the relative role of the reconstruction of the past in bringing about changes is concerned, I tried to indicate that I do not know the answer to that question. I think it may vary from case to case. I think it may be that the received wisdom—that only with the reconstruction of the past does a significant change take place in patients with a so-called structural alteration—is something that is seriously open to question. I think it's a subject for a great deal of further investigation.

*Arlow*: Of course, there's a lot of bad thinking that goes on in any kind of discipline and in the application of any kind of technique. The past is not wholly of itself; the past is significant only insofar as it becomes an intrusive element in the patient's current life. Otherwise we don't care about it and the patient doesn't care about it. What has been demonstrated from the study of people's lives in analysis and in psychotherapy is the persistent influence of certain organized parts of the past on the present. The broader issues have been discussed, I think, very comprehensively and definitively by Dr. Michels. There is no such thing as a present without the influence of the past; every bit of experience that we have is assimilated in terms of our previous experience, and every present moment becomes, in the next instant, part of our past and part of the dynamic alterations that take place in a person's development.

As far as the question of the reconstruction of the past, that's old hat in psychotherapy and in psychoanalysis. You don't reconstruct the past as a kind of exercise for your schoolteacher. The reconstruction of the past was important when Freud thought in terms of the tension of forgotten memories that had to be brought out. Nowadays, reconstruction of the past is the *result* of progress in treatment, and not its *cause*. In other words, when you have done well with a patient, then certain things fall into place and become comprehensible. We don't ever really reconstruct the patient's entire past; that is a myth and an illusion. We only reconstruct the vicissitudes of the patient's struggle, the patient's conflict; you don't do the whole person over. That is a mistaken illusion that we have picked up from the past. It is not pertinent to present-day psychotherapy.

*Galenson*: As I have been talking of the importance of preoedipal issues in elucidating the transference, I would like to emphasize my basic agreement, nonetheless, with Dr. Arlow that we cannot reconstruct the preoedipal period of life in the course of analysis or psychotherapy. At best—to borrow a phrase that Greenacre has used about construction—this is the way it *may* have been. However, I do think we can try to see the remnants of the influence of this early period on the oedipal phase and on the developments that ensue. I feel that this is possible, and perhaps even more so than we have known.

Question 4: *Dr. Galenson, how do you differentiate the preoedipal influence on transference formation in men and women?*

*Galenson*: The pivotal point, I believe, is that for the boy the disidentification with the mother is a task which must take place some time during the end of the second year—otherwise his own sense of masculinity is in grave jeopardy. This is in contrast with the development of the girl, who must maintain a female identification while yet separating herself, at least to some extent, from the earlier "symbiotic" relationship with the mother. From that point on—that is, from the end of the second year—development in boys is a very different process from that in girls; therefore its reflections, the style of organization, the kind of affect that one meets, are all different as we find them within the transference, and as we find them affecting the oedipal constellation and its resolution.

Question 5: *Dr. Galenson, could you say more about dealing with your patient's feelings of emptiness, worthlessness, etc. through the transference?*

*Galenson*: I believe these feelings, having to do with problems of self-esteem, particularly in women, rest mainly on the fact that what might seem to be the important layer of penis envy is simply one aspect—and perhaps the least important aspect—of earlier anxieties that it has evoked. These include anxiety about total body intactness, about various mental capacities—including intellectual effectiveness—and anxiety about object loss. For my patient, the feelings of emptiness and worthlessness contained within them all three layers of these basic anxieties, so that in the transference one had to decide at any one particular moment which was the most appropriate to approach.

I think that all of us have had the experience of making an interpretation (let us say, in relation to penis envy) that is hollow and meaningless, not only because it has become a cliché but because it doesn't address itself to the earlier anxieties upon which this penis envy is fundamentally based. When one addresses the patient's anxiety—for example, that her brain doesn't function well, or that her body is not pretty or is defective, or when the patient says, "I can't study when I'm alone because I feel that there is no one out there in the world and I'm cut off and entirely isolated"—and it is seen as a reflection of anxiety about object loss, such an interpretation gets closer to where the patient may be at that moment. (One cannot, of course, always say which particular developmental era may be foremost in the treatment, nor which particular anxiety may be stirring at any given time.)

Question 6: *My experience with developmentally arrested individuals reveals that these individuals have underdeveloped many essential psychic structures, such as the ego and the superego. Thus, I would disagree with Dr. Arlow when he poses the difficulties of these individuals as intrapsychic in nature. I would not agree with Dr. Gill either that they are entirely due to interpersonal conflicts. I would like to think of them as difficulties in early object relations expressed in later interpersonal relationships. Would the panelists comment on this?*

*Schwaber*: I think one aspect of this question that may warrant clarification is that a dichotomy seems to have been posed between the interpersonal and the intrapsychic. When Dr. Gill emphasizes the need for a systematic view of the context—the immediate context of the relationship—while concomitantly seeming to deemphasize the contribution from the past, one potential implication is that this is no longer an intrapsychic view but has become an interpersonal one—in the sense of its not being experienced intrapsychically. Perhaps this apparent dichotomization can be addressed.

*Arlow*: A very legitimate question! When our patients come to us for help, they are having trouble with themselves. They are dissatisfied with some aspect of their functioning—either they have some unpleasant feelings or they have some difficulty in getting along with others. What we usually find out in the course of treatment is that in many respects they think their problem generated from the external world but it lies within the interaction. What we can do when we treat them is to deal with their contribution to it. We cannot change a patient's world; we can't undo real events or unfortunate circumstances. We can try to transform the disequilibrium that has developed as the cost of the patient's attempt to adjust to both inner and outer forces.

There is a much more important issue which is implicit in the question, having to do with pathogenesis. What the question directs itself to, as I see it, is that there are certain difficulties that arise in the course of an individual's very early development—either developmental defects of certain ego functions, or perhaps some inherent inability to relate to others. These difficulties may be congenitally determined, according to one school of thought, or determined by unempathic mothering or traumatic events in the first few months of life, according to another. In either case, it reflects a particular viewpoint which sees pathogenesis as deriving from very early, perhaps nonconflictual situations having to do with developmental failure either of nurturing or of development which leads to dislocation and maladaptation. I think this is a position that has not been represented in the discussion because we have been dealing primarily with therapeutic situations that focus on intrapsychic conflict. But I would certainly say that this is something that must be taken into account.

*Gill:* I agree with Dr. Arlow that this is an exceedingly difficult question, and I think any doctrinaire positions on it are bad. I think, however, it's important to point out when one discusses this issue of intrapsychic and interpersonal, that these words have become slogans, with connotations that people use to fight, instead of trying to examine the issues. An interpersonal point of view is so often taken to mean that one is, let us say, a Sullivanian and therefore superficial, doesn't understand the nature of drive, or doesn't understand that there is such a thing as intrapsychic conflict.

I also think an important distinction, as Dr. Arlow said, has to be made between what the person is like now and how he got to be what he is. From that point of view I didn't quite understand the question insofar as it spoke to a disagreement with me, because, as I understood it, there was a reference to early object relations as being very important. I would wonder how the questioner thinks of these early object relations. Do they constitute an interpersonal interaction or not?

One point of view that I would like to speak against, and that I think an emphasis on interpersonal relationships is very often misunderstood as connoting, is the idea that a human being at birth is a tabula rasa and that what determines what that human being becomes are the interpersonal relationships that he has—as if that's all there is to it. It seems to me that Freud addressed this question very clearly in what he called the "complemental series" (1917, p. 347). What a human being becomes is a result of both nature and nurture. In a very general sense, one can speak of the nurture as the interpersonal experiences to which one is subjected; at the same time there is nature, there is the biological organism—whether or not the concept of drive is the correct one for that. The issue of the cognitive capacity of an infant to understand the interpersonal environment in which he is reared must also be taken into account. I guess the main thing I am trying to say is that we have to be careful not to permit "interpersonal" and "intrapsychic" to become slogans with which we attack one another instead of examining the issues.

Question 7: *How does Greenson's concept of the "real" relationship relate to the panelists' views of transference?*

*Gill*: In a general sense, one of the difficulties with that kind of concept is that it implies that the nature of the patient's experience of the relationship can be cut up into various kinds of things: there is a real relationship, and there's the neurotic relationship; there's a distortion of the real relationship; there's this kind of alliance and that kind of alliance. There may be some conceptual advantage to be gained in that sort of cutting things up, but I think when it comes to the actual work with the patient, this effort only interferes with one's ability to empathize with what the patient is experiencing. One should just try to deal as well as one can with what the patient is presenting, trying especially, as I have tried to emphasize, to be always aware of the allusions to the patient's experience of the relationship. To cut it up into categories is a distraction that can lead, I think, to what Dr. Michels emphasized when he spoke of the need to *hear* what the patient is saying, when he cautioned us not to impose our preconceived notions onto the situation.

*Galenson*: I'm a little bit bewildered because I think that in Dr. Gill's comments there is a straw horse being erected only to be knocked down. Any contact between patient and therapist always involves, obviously, some interpersonal operations; otherwise they wouldn't be hearing one another, or there wouldn't be any kind of interaction between these two people. As far as the analyst as a real person versus the analyst as a transference figure, that too is an extremely difficult matter to delineate.

With Dr. Arlow's patient, I would begin to see myself as a transference figure even earlier than he did. I think that before the telephone call was made, as she was carrying around that slip of paper, somehow he had begun to have a meaning—maybe not the meaning of him as he is in his present form, but in some fantasy form there was a Dr. Arlow on that slip of paper to whom that patient was already reacting. We all have that experience of having people come to us for a variety of reasons—perhaps women tend to have more of that these days because we are being sought out by many women patients as the magical source of identification and rapid transformation. (Indeed, many of us, I believe, have to then deal with some very difficult areas because the demandingness and the infantile qualities often surface more rapidly with a woman therapist.) Although the reality of the sex of the therapist may evoke a difference in terms of the patient's initial reaction, I do not feel that in the long run this early difference matters. Similar material will come up in relation to a man, but with different timing. With a woman therapist, for example, patients may present initially in far more regressed fashion, and one must be wary of the often rather false picture of pathology which they evoke.

There are, then, many ways in which the person of the therapist plays a role, but these are part of the entire gamut of transference reactions. What is particularly important is that we recognize that somewhere in all these reactions there *have* to be reflections of the primordial relation to the mother. My own experience in working with infants has been most helpful in sharpening my ability to be aware of these very early transferences. It is an experience I strongly advocate, for it promotes a certain kind of empathy with the behavior of a young child and an ability to see certain patterns of organization which are very helpful in understanding adult patients.

*Arlow*: I agree with Dr. Gill's views on the real relationship with the analyst. You can't cut up the relationship; you try to analyze or understand or deal with those aspects of the interaction that become significant or useful for the patient to understand. Behind all of this is always the real idea that the patient has come because you profess to be able to help him and have assumed a second set of responsibilities toward him.

Let me illustrate how these things work with two examples: One is borrowed from Dr. Loewenstein, who used this example to point out how the correct interpretation given at the wrong time can be useless. This has to do with a very narcissistic patient who always demanded that she be the center of attention. She felt she didn't get enough attention when she was a child and she was going on like this for a long time. Her analyst dozed off, his cigar fell onto the carpet, the carpet began to burn, the smoke began to rise, the patient smelled it, turned and looked around, and said, "Doctor, Doctor, wake up! Your rug is on fire and you're not even listening to me." And he said, "That's how you are. You want all the attention on you all the time." That was a violation of the real relationship.

On the other hand, I share an office with two other colleagues, one of whom is away in the morning. I sometimes go into his part of the office for supplies, an area usually kept dark in the morning; it's also right next to the bathroom. I have a patient who had a fear of burglars from the time he was three and a half. He is terrified of being assaulted and of any noises in the night. He happens to be six-foot-three and swims a hundred laps in an Olympic-sized pool every day. One time when he was coming out of the bathroom and I was coming from the darkened office, he suddenly saw me and had the idea I was going to pounce on him and destroy him. Well, that's very unreal—that's transference.

Question 8: *Dr. Arlow, how do you distinguish between character structure and transference? How is this illustrated in your patient?*

*Arlow*: Character structure and transference are related in this fundamental aspect—namely, they are both the outcome of a certain kind of conflict. Character structure represents a way in which a set of defensive maneuvers instituted to control a particular conflict becomes crystallized as part of the typical, ordinary reactive pattern of the individual's relationship to others. Somebody could be very meticulous, let us say, as a reaction formation against being assaultive and insulting.

With a transference, the character structure can be applied in a very defensive way, the stronger the impulses to do the opposite come up. What appears as character structure in ordinary relations can, in the transference, become a very strongly needed, repetitive pattern used to keep hostile impulses in check. In the case of my patient, one part of her character structure seemed to be in relationship to men, to get them involved in all kinds of anticipations and to let them down; and, of course, I think I illustrated that she was doing the same thing to me.

*Schwaber*: To continue then, with the previous question about the nature of the relationship between the transference and the real, I think that one implication in the recurrence of this dilemma, perhaps bearing on its ambiguity, is that there lies beyond it a further question: "real" from whose point of view? Is "real" what is real as defined by the therapist or is it "real" as defined by the patient? That may be where some of the continuing controversy lies.

*Gill*: I think Dr. Schwaber handled that question of the real relationship better than I did, and I will elaborate on that. In my opinion, there is a very significant difference of opinion here. I do not agree with Dr. Galenson that I was erecting a straw man. One of the things that I frequently hear after I present the point of view I have presented is that there is nothing so unique about what I am saying—that it is, after all, a very widely held point of view. And I just don't think so! I think there is a basic difference of opinion here, which doesn't emerge because the very idea that what the *therapist does* relates to the patient's experience of the relationship is so obvious that it would seem that everyone must agree to it and what's all the fuss about?

The fuss, I think, pivots around a central epistemological question having to do with what is the nature of the reality—in this case, the reality of an interpersonal relationship. That is why I said Dr. Schwaber's answer to this question of the real relationship was better than mine. She said, " 'Real' from whose point of view?" In that sense she was saying there is one epistemological position that says there is a reality and we can discern what it is; there is another that says there is no absolute reality. Reality, however painful a conclusion that may be, is relative. In our work with patients our primary attention is to try to understand *their* position on reality. Ultimately, we hope that they will come to see that their position on reality is not an unequivocal one, that there are other possible interpretations. The way will then be opened for their beginning to realize it is possible to change what they formerly held as certain very rigid points of view.

*Arlow*: I want to add a note of agreement in extension to what Dr. Gill has just said. The fact is that neither psychoanalysis nor any system of psychotherapy has a claim on the epistemologically significant reality. Freud was very circumspect as to what he spoke about in connection with reality; its assessment reflected the ability to distinguish external perception from inner fantasy.

As far as any judgment about the nature of *real* events in the world, what events *really* mean, what other people's intentions *really* are, what is the *realistic* thing to do—we have no claim to any kind of expertise or definitive word on that. The realities that a person has to face are quite different from the kind of realities with which a psychotherapist can deal. He or she can explicate a situation and point out possible consequences of different paths of behavior to a patient, but without any claim to a superior knowledge as to what should be done or what is the real nature of the events in the external world transpiring at a particular time.

*Galenson*: I will just conclude briefly by commenting that I agree with Dr. Gill that I think there *is* a difference of opinion here—and an important one—but not in the area that I had mentioned before. The difference of opinion that I have with Dr. Gill has to do with the emphasis he places on the here and now at the cost of the past, and I hope for a future opportunity to discuss this matter.

## REFERENCE

Freud, S. (1917), Some thoughts on development and regression—aetiology. *Standard Edition*, 16: 339–357. London: Hogarth Press, 1963.

# 10

# Responses to Introductory Questions

Question 1: *Is transference a phenomenon to be understood entirely within the intrapsychic realm, or, since it is experienced within the context of a relationship, thus taking on an interpersonal meaning, does this leave some measure of ambiguity as to whether we are including in our purview a realm of experience outside the intrapsychic domain?*

*Michels*: Dr. Schwaber poses some paradoxes and dilemmas for us. I believe that they provide useful starting points for a series of dialectics. Of course, like most dilemmas that initiate dialectics they may collapse upon further study rather than be resolved one way or the other.

This first question relates to the tension between the intrapsychic and the interpersonal views of transference. Some of Freud's followers had a particular interest in transference viewed as an aspect of the therapeutic relationship that might be detected in the therapist rather than transference as an aspect of the patient's mental life. However, when these are posed as opposites there is an implication that an interpersonal life exists which is distinct from intrapsychic life, that there is a life of the mind and a separate life between people, and that one of these might exist independently of the other. I believe that the exploration of that paradox would lead to the recognition that intrapsychic and interpersonal aspects of transference are two aspects of a single phenomenon.

*Valenstein*: Transference is a phenomenon which is both interpersonal and intrapsychic. It originates in formative experience with early objects, that is, the mother-child experience, and continues on into more evolved and complex interpersonal events, experiences, and impressions, including the pivotal triadic oedipal situation, its unfolding, consolidation, and resolution. In these respects, it reflects the sequence and vicissitudes of development, both normal and neurotic.

Intrapsychically, transference refers to the interplay between past and present and to the significance which early impressions and events hold for the future, as they are laid down in memory traces and conflicts. Subject to the principle of the repetition compulsion, they are endlessly recapitulated in derivative improvisations in the here and now.

*Ornstein*: Each of Dr. Schwaber's questions penetrates to the core of psychoanalysis. As I read and reread them, it seemed I could not venture a brief response to any of them, because I would inevitably leave important points untouched. These questions brought home to me again how in psychoanalysis each question is closely related to the other, as must then be the case with each answer. Psychoanalysis (whichever version of it we may have in mind) seems to make most sense in its totality. Fragments of it—individual answers to individual questions—are always open to misunderstanding and are always in need of endless qualifications. With this preamble I shall accept the risk of responding briefly.

The key issue in this first question relates to the word

"entirely." Both of Freud's original definitions —the spatial and the temporal images, as Dr. Schwaber described them—essentially portray transference as emerging entirely from within. The external or interpersonal stimulus is viewed as insignificant; this is so because it is felt to be easily interchangeable, and further, because it serves merely as a vehicle to bring forth the same feelings, wishes, or attitudes that are already "deposited" in the unconscious in their particular configuration, determined by early experience.

The clinical and theoretical problems that arise from this viewpoint are legion, with many efforts at their solution in the literature; I cannot even begin to address them in this context. Suffice it to say that increasing recognition of the significance of the "interpersonal" aspects of transference only added to these difficulties. Such concepts as "therapeutic alliance," "working alliance," and especially the "real relationship"—as split off from the transference — justifiably raise the question: "Is there a realm of experience [in the treatment process] outside the intrapsychic domain?"

Sidestepping the important issue of whether the psyche is a closed or an open system, I view the psychoanalytic process as a unitary experience in an intersubjective field (see, for example, Stolorow, Brandchaft, and Atwood, 1983) in which the "interpersonal" can be viewed only from the vantage point of each participant's inner experience. Thus, each person's—patient's and analyst's—experience of the other falls within his or her respective intrapsychic domains. It is here that Kohut's new concept of the selfobject encompasses the "external stimulus" within the patient's own psychic reality—that is, intrapsychically. From such a vantage point, therefore, there is no realm of experience in the analytic situation that is outside the intrapsychic domain.

*Galenson*: Since transference is expressed within the context of a current relationship, it reflects both earlier relationships and aspects of the current relationship as well. In both instances, transference refers to intrapsychic events, of course, and not to behavioral aspects either of the past or the present.

*Gill*: There is no "ambiguity as to whether we are including in our purview a realm of experience outside the intrapsychic domain." We are definitely doing so. The central point of my paper is that a solely intrapsychic view of transference is a conceptual abstraction. Any particular transference manifestation takes place in an interpersonal context and is therefore influenced to varying degrees by that context.

*Arlow*: I shall include in my answer some general statements about my views on the theory of transference. I regard transference as a universal phenomenon that occurs inside and outside the analytic situation. It has a special technical significance in analysis. It arises as a compromise formation and as a derivative expression of a persistent unconscious conflict over a wish from childhood. The wish is expressed concretely at some level of mental experience in the form of an unconscious fantasy. The fantasy integrates wish, defense, superego influence, etc. Derivatives of the unconscious fantasy appear in different forms, consciously and unconsciously, in the course of development. What happens in transference is that the particular individual who is the transference object is cast in a role by the patient in keeping with some inner scenario. As I have stated on other occasions, the plot of the scenario remains the same while the characters and the locale change as the individual grows and matures. In the transference a persistent unconscious wish from childhood directed toward an *object* is transformed into a pattern of behavior and thinking concerning a *person*. This is the bridge between the intrapsychic, which concerns objects, and the interpersonal, which concerns people (see Arlow, 1980).

The analytic situation does not create the transference. Transference is not a set of special regressive phenomena induced by being a patient, by lying down, by having someone give undivided attention, or by baring one's secrets in an unbalanced, unequal way. Any of these factors or all of them may be significant provided they have some resonance with the patient's basic unconscious fantasy and that they reflect some specific, not general, aspect of the patient's personal mental history. What can be reconstructed in the transference is only what is persistently active as a dynamic force in the person's mind. For this reason, transference really cannot be used as a basis for reconstructing the entirety of the individual's history. What it does enable us to do is to reconstruct the vicissitudes of the patient's struggle with his conflictual unconscious wishes. In other words, in analysis we study in the transference the transformations of the neurotic process during the course of a lifetime.

Question 2: *As corollary to Question 1, is the transference a distortion, a product of the patient's emerging wishes and defenses projected onto the image of the therapist or analyst—a distortion requiring ultimate correction—or is this a judgment not to be made? Is it rather to be viewed and articulated as a perception formed by the intervention of the therapist (or analyst) as this interweaves with and influences, in turn, the inner experience of the patient? Does the past and how it is represented distort the present, or does the present re-create and create anew the shifting imagery of the past?*

*Michels*: In response to this question, I believe again that the tension between these views—whether transference involves a distortion requiring correction or a perception or judgment that is not to be assessed as right or wrong—disappears if one recognizes that implicit in posing them as alternatives is the notion that some kinds of human perception exist that do not involve distortion. When we realize that there are no such experiences, we see transference as simply one kind of distortion among the many that are intrinsic to the process of perception.

*Valenstein*: Again, this is not an either-or: the influence of the past to distort the present or of present perception and experience to possibly distort memories and/or to create fantasies of the past. As Nunberg wrote in 1951, the "Janus" which is transference is "two-faced, with one face turned to the past, the other to the present. Through transference the patient lives the present in the past and the past in the present" (p. 5). Moreover, this is an active process. For the intention, as it were, is that the object of transference, upon whom are projected fantasies and expectations originating out of the past of the patient, respond reciprocally in kind but within the context of the patient's contemporary life. He or she is expected to confirm the current reality of the transference *assignment*, and is so perceived.

The transference figure is played upon, ployed in effect, toward an interpersonal verification of the transference predisposition—that it is not only subjectively true, but objectively valid. Once experientially validated, it follows that a patient's characteristic ways of adapting, of coping and dealing with conflict, of gratifying himself or herself are legitimized for ongoing reenactment in the here and now. However, insofar as past and present can be disentangled toward the *knowing* of what is the contribution from the past and what the influence of the present, then the patient might be less under the unconscious sway of the heretofore unknown past, whether in fact or fantasy, and more in a position to live the present in its own right.

*Ornstein:* It follows from my emphasis upon the patient's psychic reality that what the external observer (centered on his or her own reality) might view as a distortion, the introspective (empathic) observer (centered on the patient's reality) would, indeed, view "as a perception formed by the intervention of the therapist (or analyst) as it interweaves with and influences, in turn, the inner experience of the patient." From this latter view, it is not that the past is represented in the distortion of the present, but rather it is "the present which re-create(s) and create(s) anew the shifting imagery of the past." The key point is that this new creation includes the therapist's contributions through his or her interventions, the significance of which we can only know from the way the patient experienced it—that is, from within the intrapsychic domain. Hence, in further response to Question 1: while transference does not entirely originate from within, the therapist's contributions are formatively significant—*with the concept of the selfobject, the experiencing of the transference is to be understood entirely within the intrapsychic realm.*

*Galenson:* I believe a degree of distortion always characterizes the transference, the past distorts the present, and the present realigns the memories and perceptions of the past. Furthermore, the past is subject to distortion simply by virtue of the fact that the past is viewed from the adult perspective rather than reexperienced as it was in childhood. As the mental apparatus matures it colors childhood experiences by virtue of this change alone.

*Gill:* Transference is not a distortion in any simple sense of the word, even in apparently grossly maladaptive responses. It is, indeed, an experience jointly contributed to by both participants in however varying proportions and therefore always has a degree of plausibility; that is, it is understandable in terms of the current interpersonal context.

*Arlow*: The transference phenomena represent just another set of manifestations of the neurotic process to the extent that the effects of persistent unconscious fantasies intrude upon interpersonal relations in the treatment as they do in the course of the neurosis. Transference represents another example of the distortion of perception and reaction introduced by means of the intrusion of unconscious fantasy into conscious experience. By interpreting the transference the analyst enables the patient to distinguish between fantasy and reality, between past and present. The analyst does not ''correct'' transference distortion through confrontation and explanation of reality. What the analyst does is interpret the intrusion of the effects of the unconscious fantasy into the patient's perceptions and responsiveness. As I have written in my papers on unconscious fantasy (Arlow, 1969a, b), it is the past distorting the present as a result of the effects of the mental set created by the persistent unconscious fantasy. This applies just as well to the personal myth, which is a recasting, distorting, reediting of one's past in terms of a persistent unconscious fantasy.

Question 3: *As further corollary, is the transference to be relinquished on the path to psychic maturity or is it to remain part of an ongoing process influencing the continuity of development throughout life? Is it primarily an aspect of neurosis, a mark of immaturity, or is it a part of all life experience, a component of its depth and meaningfulness?*

*Michels*: I think this dilemma can be paraphrased: Is the goal of treatment, the meaning of psychological health or psychoanalytic cure, a life without infantile themes, emotional conflicts, unconscious mental processes, or the impact of past experiences on the person? I will say no more.

*Valenstein*: Loewald, in particular, has emphasized the normative developmental impact of transference, in pointing out the transferential potential of self-object experience. As he put it (Valenstein, 1974), "Not only do early object ties materially determine the nature of later ones 'by transference,' but later object ties—in our context especially those intense ones which become established in the analytic relationship—have their impact, 'by transference,' on the revival, mode of reexperiencing and restructuring of the infantile object ties" (p. 312). In that same panel, I noted that the issue was that not "*everything* is necessarily transference that happens emotionally between patient and analyst, or between any two human beings, for that matter. Although it is true that there are increments of the inchoate past in every relationship, bringing these elements within the usual clinical domain of transference so broadens the term that it begins to lose some of its psychoanalytic and technical specificity" (p. 313).

*Ornstein*: As long as the transference was viewed predominantly as a distortion, as an archaic remnant of an infantile neurosis surviving in adult neurosis, it made sense to expect its diminution and ultimate relinquishment on the way toward psychic maturity—a view with which I disagree. I see transference as ubiquitous, indeed part of all life experience, a component of its depth and meaningfulness, and part of an ongoing process influencing the continuity of development throughout life.

*Galenson*: I believe transference remains part of everyone's psychological life, part of the functioning of the mental apparatus. Furthermore, neurosis is universal, and transference phenomena are part and parcel of this universal human characteristic.

*Gill*: Freud clearly defined transference as both pathological and nonpathological. He called the latter the unobjectionable positive transference. The transference neuroses were so named to emphasize not the maladaptive nature of transference but the capacity to enter a meaningful and workable human relationship. Even if only in nuance, all our patterns of interpersonal relationship—that is, transference—are, as Freud put it, our particular ways of loving and, as we would now add, hating.

*Arlow*: Transferences are never relinquished in the course of life. All our experiences are metaphorically assimilated and integrated with the past in keeping with the criteria of likeness or difference. Therefore, there are some reverberations of the past in every new perception and in every new relationship. What is significant is the extent to which the effects of unconscious wishes intrude upon and distort the perception, interpretation, and response to the present experience. Accordingly, transference is not a mark of neurosis per se. It is a universal tendency which becomes intensely pronounced in the neurosis and especially in the analytic situation. The conditions of the psychoanalytic situation permit the neurotic conflict to emerge during the psychoanalytic process in clearer focus and with much greater intensity. This is so because the derivative expressions of the unconscious fantasy emerge undiluted by distracting interpersonal relations and undistorted by realistic interactions.

Question 4: *Is the transference but a single facet of the totality of the patient's experience within the clinical situation, a facet to be differentiated from such aspects as the therapeutic alliance or the real relationship? If so, is the transference in some sense not real, and is there a reality that does not include transference?*

*Michels*: I believe that this problem—is transference only one facet of a totality of the relationship to be differentiated from the therapeutic alliance?—more than the others, reduces to an issue of preferred definition. Some definitions differentiate transference from therapeutic alliance while others treat therapeutic alliance as an aspect of transference phenomena. I have been using transference to include what is called therapeutic alliance. However, I believe that one might differentiate psychoanalysis from psychoanalytically informed psychotherapy in part by discussing to what extent the therapeutic alliance aspects of the transference are subject to exploration and inquiry and to what extent they are left unanalyzed.

*Valenstein*: As already discussed, not all that transpires within the clinical situation, or between patient and therapist, is necessarily transference, although by reason of the richly integrated overdetermination of psychic events and behavior, transference aspects or contributions, more or less so, are not to be excluded; nor is the concept of a basic or primary transference extraneous to the concept of the therapeutic alliance, or the real relationship. In fact, as I discussed the matter in my presentation, ''the viability of a therapy depends upon a fundamental confidence transference. . . . [implying] mutuality, which is in turn ascribable to the continuity of basic trust and the potential for growth through identification—qualities which emerge out of the developmental matrix of the early mother-child relationship.''

*Ornstein*: As I stated in response to Question 1, such ''part'' experience as therapeutic alliance or the real relationship cannot (and need not) be separated from the totality of the analytic experience. Postulating a separate domain of "real experience" gets us into the sort of difficulties indicated by the question, "Is the transference in some sense not real, and is there a reality that does not include transference?" Of course transference is real—though it refers to the patient's reality and not the analyst's. There is no reality for the patient that does not include his or her transference.

*Galenson*: The therapeutic alliance, or rather the patient's capacity to form a therapeutic alliance, depends upon the nature of the patient's transference. As for the question of reality, there is, of course, a reality that does not include transference, but then transference experiences are quite "real" to the patient.

*Gill*: The patient's experience of the relationship is a totality within which different facets can be separated off only conceptually. While some facets may be considered unrealistic, though surely not unreal, a judgment that a particular aspect of the patient's experience is unrealistic can be made only within the context of recognizing that it nevertheless has a degree of plausibility, as I described in response to the second question. There is no realistic experience without transference and no transference without a realistic aspect.

*Arlow*: I find it difficult to answer this question as it is posed. There are many facets to the patient's experience within a clinical situation. What the analyst interprets are the distortions introduced by the transference. The concepts of therapeutic alliance and the "real" relationship, I think, are misconceptions and confusions that tend to blur the concept of transference. Also, of course, there is a reality that does not include transference. It is a constant factor operative in both parties in the analytic situation. Somewhere in the back of his mind, unless the patient is truly psychotic, he is always aware of the fact that he is going through the analysis in order to be helped by means of a certain technique to which he is expected to conform.

Question 5: *How do we understand the varieties of transferences other than the oedipal—the preoedipal transference, the primal or basic transference, or the selfobject transference, in which the analyst or therapist may be experienced as not entirely separate from ego or self? Have these varieties the same conceptual meaning as transference to a differentiated object?*

*Michels*: This dilemma addresses the relationship between oedipal transferences and other transferences. There has never been any serious question about the existence and the clinical importance of transference phenomena stemming from a variety of developmental epochs, not just the oedipal epoch. The controversial issue is the extent to which the techniques that have become associated with psychoanalysis are applicable to the exploration and interpretation of transferences from all developmental epochs and to what extent they are specific for transferences that stem from phases of development in which the child's experience has been organized into a relatively stable and differentiated world and encoded and preserved by symbols. In other words, to what extent can the verbal and symbolic techniques that are usually thought to be central to psychoanalysis be used in exploring transference phenomena that stem from preverbal or presymbolic epochs of development? There seems to be agreement that, in general, earlier presymbolic experiences are often activated in transference relationships, and that they may become central to the therapeutic process. Furthermore, this is more likely to occur with certain groups

of patients, including those with more serious psychopathology. Treatment is helpful to such patients, and an
understanding of their transference themes is a valuable
guide in such treatment. The therapist's use of that understanding often involves a range of responses and interventions wider than the interpretive approach that characterizes
psychoanalysis. Partly as a result of this, and partly reflecting the nature of their psychopathology, these patients rarely
achieve the comprehensive understanding and resolution of
the transference that is the goal of psychoanalysis.

*Valenstein*: It is specifically those individuals who have
failed to achieve consistent self-realization, separate from
the *other*, from the primary object, who remain significantly
fixated to a "selfobject transference, in which the analyst
or therapist may be experienced as not entirely separate
from ego or self." Their transference predilection, especially as they may regress in the therapeutic situation, is
quite different than transference to a differentiated object.
As I wrote earlier, "Since the major disturbance in self and
object relations constitutes an early developmental defect
in ego structure, psychoanalytic interpretations [i.e., articulate explanations at a predominantly cognitive-cognated
level of communication, which, after all, cannot really reach
the primary process preverbal/earliest verbal level of development, are nonmutative and relatively ineffective in
their context]" (1973, p. 390). "If they are to mean anything, they have to resonate with the immediate essential
transactional experiential elements in the therapeutic situation" (1979, pp. 131–132).

*Ornstein*: The fundamental paradigm of the oedipal transference assumes that an essentially well-differentiated, well-
delineated, hence separate and more or less autonomous
person (the patient) will perceive the analyst as a well-dif-

ferentiated, well-delineated, separate and autonomous object—onto whom will be projected infantile, drive-related wishes and fantasies, with their defensive and anachronistic distortions. This formulation is the result of certain basic assumptions about neurosogenesis and, more important, of a particular observational mode which had served us reasonably well with healthier, neurotic patients—or so we thought, at least prior to the era of the widening scope of psychoanalysis.

When it was finally recognized that preoedipal needs, wishes, fantasies, and demands (and the archaic defenses against them) entered analyses with increasing frequency, they were at first viewed as regressively coloring the core of the oedipal transference, which was ultimately to emerge to full view. However, these more archaic elements blurred the hitherto clear outlines of the classical transference neurosis—with a call for more radical reconceptualizations, that is, those not constrained by the absolute primacy of the oedipus complex in neurosogenesis. These were slow in forthcoming. The term "preoedipal transference," for instance, remained theoretically and clinically ambiguous. First, it did not aid in differentiating regression from the oedipus complex from fixation prior to reaching it developmentally—when that difference was thought to be crucial in relation to analyzability. Second, it offered little added analytic-therapeutic leverage—rather, the primacy of drive-defense interpretations was retained, irrespective of whether the preoedipal issues originated in regression or fixation. It is in relation to these clinical and theoretical problems that the conceptions of the archaic selfobject first brought a distinct, radical advance.

As to the primal or basic transference—considered a prerequisite for analysis—this serves as the archaic source of the basic trust in the analyst's benevolent attitude. This transference originates in the conflict-free sphere of the mind, the sphere of progressive neutralization. It is, therefore, a transference only in the temporal sense—based broadly on (optimal) past experiences—and not in the spatial sense, since it does not emerge from behind a repression barrier; its source is not in the conflictual, divided segment of the psyche.

Oedipal, preoedipal, and basic transferences are formulations that conceive of the individual without his context. The selfobject concept, on the other hand, by definition takes the context into consideration. The selfobject transference does not refer to a lack of perceptual differentiation, or a lack of cognitive grasp of separateness in time and space; rather it speaks to the specific meaning the analyst or therapist has for the patient as part of the patient's self-experience. From this observational vantage point the analyst (or therapist) is always a selfobject—archaic or more mature, depending upon the specific psychic functions he serves for the patient.

*Galenson*: I favor the view that there are many aspects of the transference which derive from the preoedipal era and, as such, would bring a very different quality than the oedipal aspects. This is so not only because of incomplete self-object differentiation but because of the instability of the self-image and of the object representation of that early era.

*Gill*: I shall not attempt to define the several varieties of transference referred to in the question, but I do believe they all deserve to be regarded as forms of transference. That is not the same as saying they have "the same conceptual meaning as transference to a differentiated object." I should also note the distinction made by Kohut between a cognitively and an affectively differentiated object, recognizing that those terms too are polar abstractions.

*Arlow*: The answer to this question may be seen as a corollary to what I have said earlier about the distinction between the person and the object. In the course of the analysis the therapist may come to be regarded unconsciously by the patient as representing some object of infantile wishes. The object may be the patient's own self, body, body part, another person, part of another person, or an inanimate thing (I avoid using the term "object" here because I want to restrict that term now to its technical analytic sense). But the important element is to keep distinct the idea of object and person. In analyzing the transference, as in analyzing anything else in the course of treatment, we must delineate the nature of the unconscious fantasy and define the aim or wish expressed and the object that would fulfill that wish or upon which that wish may be discharged. The concept of transference is the same whether the analyst or therapist, in fantasy, represents a person from the past, the patient's phallus—real or imaginary—or an old blanket or other so-called transitional object to which the patient used to cling.

Question 6: *How do we integrate the findings of the infant researcher—data derived from direct observation—into our understanding of transference? As we know, transference (in Freud's clinical usage) was discovered and articulated in the analytic situation, from which a history of development was subsequently derived. What are the implications for the understanding of transference if this process proceeds in the reverse direction—if, from the observation of infants and children, the attempt is made to infer intrapsychic meaning? Is it possible to bridge the leap of inference that must be made here?*

*Michels*: This question speaks to the relationship between research data derived from the direct observation of infants and our clinical studies. Dr. Schwaber says that we have constructed a history of development from our clinical studies, and that now our infant observers have given us information about the developmental events of childhood. I would suggest that what we actually construct in our clinical work is not a history of development but a myth of genesis. Our infant researches provide us a history of development, and the question should be formulated as: what is the significance of a history of development to a myth of genesis? I do not think that they are irrelevant, but I also do not think that we can evaluate a myth simply by comparing it to the data of historical or archeological research. Myths, after all, are created for purposes other than preserving the facts of history.

Myths may be inspired by history, and models for genetic reconstruction may be inspired by the developmental observations of infant researchers. However, this is a source of inspiration, not a system of scientific deduction or a method of validation. We are reconstructing our patients' memories of their inner worlds, and infant researchers have even less access to the inner world of infants than we have to the inner world of adults. Our constructions from adult memories and derivatives must overcome the problem of time, but they remain in the domain of subjective experiences. The infant researcher makes inferences that refer to the immediate situation, but these require a leap from the world of observation to the inner world of subjective experience. The approaches are different, and they can enrich each other, but problems generated in one domain cannot be solved by inquiry in the other.

*Valenstein*: True, transference was inferred from the treatment of neurotic adults who recapitulated, so it seemed, conflicts and patterns of response to the analyst reminiscent of what apparently had prevailed or appeared to have occurred, according to the patient's recollections of early years. In other words, "hysterics suffer mainly from reminiscences'' (Freud, 1895, p. 7), and they also repeat these reminiscences in the transference neurosis.

Perhaps the first validation through direct observation of infants of the nexus of transference, as well as mastery through the ego aspect of the repetition compulsion, came with Freud's description (1920, pp. 14–15) of his grandson's playing out the going and the return of his mother in the game of ''o-o-o-o'' and ''da'' (a forerunner of Mahler's formulation of the ''rapprochement'' subphase). Correlating data regarding development, including those concerning transference, from direct observation of infants and children with retrospective inferences arrived at through the observation and treatment of adults is a two-way street, serving to inform and validate each.

*Ornstein*: This question is as yet unsettled. It may, however, be said tentatively—and in order to articulate a principle—that the findings of the infant researchers have no direct bearing upon our understanding of the transference. If transference is the result of the amalgamation and intrapsychic elaboration of present experience, influenced by the ever-changing configuration of the subjective past, then it is only the observation of the patient in that intersubjective field that presents relevant data for our understanding of the transference. The question still remains, however, how is the analyst affected by knowledge derived from direct observation of infants or, better yet, infants and their mothers together? The comparison of the data of reconstruction and of direct observation has an important bearing on psychoanalytic theory in general and on our view of psychopathology in particular. Its impact on the understanding of transference—and hence as a contribution to technique—is uncertain, but we must be wary of reading something into the transference experience based on configurations formulated in direct observation, rather than reading something "out of it."

*Galenson*: The leap from the data of direct infant observational research to aspects of transference manifestations is an enormous one, particularly since we *infer* from behavioral manifestations in the infant what *may be* the underlying psychological processes of these behaviors. Yet without this inference and an empathic approach to infant material, we would return to behaviorism—a fruitless pursuit. My own approach to adult psychoanalytic material has included searching for clusters and patterns of defenses and conflicts which have some basic similarity to those found during infancy.

*Gill*: It is indeed a leap from observations on infants to conjectures about their intrapsychic state. Although all psychoanalytic observations include both introspection (vicarious) and extrospection (to use the terms employed by Kohut), the ambiguity as to their relative roles becomes particularly great in infant observation. In such research conclusions allegedly based on extrospection may, in fact, lean heavily on unrecognized introspection. Research on preverbal subjects is most hazardous in this respect, though nevertheless, it is important. Trained and qualified observers and converging lines of evidence provide some safeguards.

As for the implications for transference, the greatest danger lies in the genetic fallacy—that is, in the assumption that pathology in the adult is either regression to or fixation upon infantile stages, whether normal or pathological.

*Arlow*: The answers to this question are included in my earlier remarks. One must not confuse knowledge of developmental stages and subsequent psychopathological formations as if the latter were direct, conflict-free expressions of the former. I think there is tremendous confusion introduced at this point in psychoanalysis by the uncritical transposition of observational data onto later transference or neurotic manifestations.

Question 7: *How do the positions taken on these questions influence the interpretive process? What do we interpret? Some will argue that only interpretations bearing on the experiential immediacy of the transference are efficacious; others feel that interpretations relating to broader aspects of the patient's experience may be meaningful as well.*

*Michels*: The question of what to interpret, and the special role of transference interpretations, are central to the theory of psychotherapy. In general, we think of the patient's experience of an interpretation as well as the therapist's intent. From the patient's point of view all interpretations are to some extent transference interpretations, insofar as they are an inherent part of the ongoing therapeutic process, and must therefore bear on "the experiential immediacy of the transference." However, this is not always the focus of the manifest content of the interpretations. Furthermore, we understand individual interpretations as components of a more complex structure. A single interpretation may speak to the patient's current life, early development, or the therapeutic relationship and the transference. However, as the treatment progresses, these individual interpretations should come to form a larger interpretive process. Psychoanalytic psychotherapy always involves the therapist's recognition of the role of transference themes in this larger process. Usually this recognition is explicit, although from time to time—particularly in some briefer and more supportive psychotherapies—the therapist may not find it helpful to draw explicit attention to transference issues. In most cases of psychoanalytic psychotherapy the transference is discussed

explicitly whenever it seems to be serving important resistive functions. In more exploratory psychotherapies nonresistant transference themes are investigated as well. In
psychoanalysis the transference is always a major theme of
the explicit interpretive process, although it is never the
only theme and the analyst should never feel constrained
to make every individual interpretive statement a "transference interpretation."

*Valenstein*: My answers to the previous questions, particularly Question 5, are relevant to the issue of the efficacy
or limitations of interpretation depending upon the nature
of the prevalent transference. This correlates with the level
of the condition under treatment—whether it is a structural
neurosis (predominantly originating in intrapsychic conflict,
postverbally) or a developmental neurosis (predominantly
narcissistic and rooted in and toward the preverbal period).

If interpretation is understood to mean appropriate
"verbal interventions of an explanatory nature which in
timing, form, and specificity seem correct in the context of
the analytic data as they have been evolving" (Valenstein,
1973, p. 365), then it follows, in my opinion, that "most
patients who are borderline, like those who are severely
narcissistic, are also relatively inaccessible to interpretation
and to the insight that correct interpretation intends, during
at least a prolonged earlier phase of their treatment. The
treatment of such conditions during a lengthy [psycho-
therapeutic] preanalytic phase has to be paramountly experiential and developmentally reparative insofar as possible"
(Valenstein, 1979, p. 131).

*Ornstein*: This is perhaps the most difficult of the questions
posed. It has to do with our view of the relation between
theory and practice. There is no theory-free observation and
therefore no theory-free intervention. Yet if we divide the

interpretive process into two conceptually distinct (though often inseparable) steps of understanding and explaining, the former is relatively less theory-laden than the latter. Formal, systematic theory—even our metapsychology—more visibly and more definitively influences the step of explaining. We explain in terms of our theories of psychopathology and we choose what and when to explain on the basis of our theory of cure. A comprehensive survey of contemporary psychoanalytic and psychotherapeutic practices would show, I believe, how profoundly we all are influenced by the theories we hold, explicitly or implicitly. Although we often hear it said that "we may disagree on theory, but we all do more or less the same thing clinically," my own experience has taught me otherwise. Case reports and discussions with colleagues buttress my assumption.

*Galenson*: Interpretations bearing on currently experienced aspects of the transference usually have a more effective impact, as most analysts eventually discover. Yet it is most valuable to attempt to go beyond this, particularly in relation to material from the preoedipal era. Some of this latter material may have to take the form of "possible or probable" reconstructions of how it might have been in the early years, since it is highly unlikely that these early experiences can be recovered as such.

*Gill*: Both here-and-now and genetic transference interpretations as well as extratransference interpretations have their place in analysis and in psychotherapy. It is my view that in terms of both immediacy and importance, transference interpretations in general and here-and-now transference interpretations in particular should have priority, not only because they provide a major basis for other types of interpretation but also because they are the more likely to be efficacious.

*Arlow*: I have answered this question—"What do we interpret?"—in some of my previous responses. Essentially we interpret the distortions introduced into the interpersonal relations as a consequence of the influence of the derivatives of the persistent unconscious fantasies of childhood. Such interpretations do not have to be made exclusively in the context of the transference. Extratransference interpretations can be and are very effective.

Question 8: *Finally, how do we translate our position on these issues from the psychoanalytic to the psychoanalytically oriented psychotherapy situation?*

*Michels*: I would prefer to rephrase the question as "What are the differences in our position on these issues in psychoanalysis as contrasted with psychoanalytically oriented psychotherapy?" This underlines that these are two different ways of applying our psychoanalytic understanding, not one real way and another dilute or translated version. They have differentiated from a common origin, and if forced to choose we would have to say that the earliest efforts of Freud and his colleagues would today be considered psychotherapy rather than psychoanalysis.

Transference phenomena are universal in all relationships, and thus in both psychoanalysis and psychotherapy. Psychoanalysts and psychoanalytically oriented therapists both try to understand the transference and to use their understanding in the treatment. The arrangements of psychoanalysis—the frequency and regularity of sessions, the couch and the analyst's anonymity—encourage a greater focus on transference themes than on those associated with outer reality. The psychotherapist is more likely to have specific therapeutic goals in mind and these, along with the arrangements and, often, the limited time, tend to shift the focus toward adaptation to external reality. In general, transference issues are explored in both types of treatment when they are associated with the analysis of resistance. In psychoanalysis, there is generally more attention to the nonresistant transferences, and there are more often interpretations aimed at making nonresistant transferences more available to exploration. Transference is an important source of compliance as well as resistance in both psychoanalysis and psychoanalytically oriented psychotherapy. In psychoanalysis the compliant transference is also explored; in psychotherapy it is more likely to be exploited in order to facilitate other therapeutic goals.

*Valenstein*: Psychoanalysis aims predominantly at insight, both currently in the derivative here and now, as well as in the past with regard to the genetic determinants of conflict and developmental mishap. Hence, in the psychoanalytic situation, transference is the instrumental means by which such insight is meaningfully achieved, inclusive of the integration of cognitive, affective, and conative components.

Psychoanalytically oriented psychotherapy, on the other hand, does not necessarily take the achievement of insight as its prime therapeutic objective, although it does depend upon clinical formulations and interventions based on psychoanalytic understanding. By reason of modifications adapting psychotherapy to the treatment of a wide variety of clinical conditions, the patient and therapist are likely to interact more flexibly along transactional lines within the context of the transference toward a pragmatically sought cumulative corrective experience in the here and now. As mentioned in my response to the previous question, this may be the most effective way of therapeutically reaching narcissistic and borderline patients. Also, it may be more expeditious for brief or intermittent therapies with limited goals. Furthermore, in such treatments it may be of the

essence that the transference be made use of at the derivative
level in the present, rather than being primarily analyzed
toward paradigmatic genetic sources, as is the intention in
the less interactive setting of psychoanalysis as such.

*Ornstein*: For me, this is the easiest question to answer, at
least in principle. As I indicated in my presentation, I view
psychoanalysis on a continuum with long-term psychoanalytic psychotherapy and with focal psychotherapy. Thus,
I can make my position clear in the following brief statement: whatever emerges in the treatment process (whatever
degree of cohesiveness the transference might attain) will
determine the depth and breadth of understanding and explaining that patient and therapist might be able to achieve
together. Since this understanding and explaining are the
essential vehicles of the complex process of treatment,
the details are a variation on the basic theme, dictated by
the setting and the patient's emerging goals in each treatment situation. In other words, what has been said here
about psychoanalysis is basically valid for psychoanalytic
psychotherapy as well.

*Galenson*: As a psychoanalytically trained and theoretically
based therapist, transference manifestations are always in
the forefront of my mind, whether in psychoanalysis or
psychotherapy. However, whether and how such transference manifestations should be interpreted depends upon the
status of the treatment situation, the nature of current defensive operations, and other related factors. The danger of
interpretation of the transference in psychotherapeutic work
is that the interpretation may be premature or too deep and
the opportunity to work it through may be inadequate.

*Gill*: My entire paper bears on the question of how we
translate our position on these issues from the psycho-

analytic to the psychoanalytic psychotherapy situation. I have argued that the view of transference and its interpretation which I advocate—its analysis in terms of the avoidance of witting suggestion and the search for and interpretation of both witting and unwitting suggestion as primary features of the technique—should be employed in a broader range of situations (defined in terms of frequency of sessions, recumbency, pathology of patient, and experience of therapist) than is ordinarily considered appropriate for psychoanalysis. Therapy in this broader range of conditions is called psychotherapy by those who insist that analytic technique can be employed only in circumstances defined relatively narrowly in terms of the dimensions I have mentioned. I disagree. I define psychotherapy as a technique which allows witting suggestion to a greater or lesser degree, that is, which deliberately permits transference that the therapist recognizes and the patient does not—or that the patient at least is unwilling to deal with explicitly—to remain unanalyzed. I refer to the long run, not the short run, of a therapy; I mean that the therapist is not obliged in my definition to deal with a transference as soon as he or she recognizes it for the therapy to qualify as analytic.

*Arlow*: This is a matter of skill and art. The issues are the same. The difficulties in psychoanalytic psychotherapy are enormously aggravated by any number of factors to which I have referred in the concluding section of my chapter. These factors involve the relative infrequency of sessions in psychoanalytic psychotherapy. The limitations are in the process of free association and the physical setting of confrontation of the patient and therapist. The therapist must perforce be more active and more certain in grasping the nature of the unconscious fantasy, the derivative manifestations of which are being actualized in the transference relationship. It becomes of utmost importance to focus on this essential feature. What the therapist does is to try to make the patient aware of the various forms which derivatives of unconscious fantasy thinking may assume. These forms may include symptoms, dreams, daydreams, or parapraxes. Transference has to be interpreted as another derivative expression of the unconscious fantasy. Thus in the case presented, at an appropriate time it would be necessary to point out to this patient how the difficulties in setting an appointment, in having her come on time, in getting clear and direct information from her, constituted expressions of her hostility toward the therapist and of her wish to frustrate and antagonize him, as she had indeed done the same to previous therapists and to her boyfriend. In effect, she had transferred her wish to destroy her boyfriend (brother, father, or doctors) onto the therapist and she has been living out such derivative manifestations of her unconscious fantasy on practically all the important men in her life. Particularly in psychoanalytic psychotherapy, any attempt to view transference as other than a derivative of an unconscious fantasy will blur the nature of the therapeutic interaction.

## REFERENCES

Arlow, J.A. (1969a), Unconscious fantasy and disturbances of conscious experience. *Psychoanal. Quart.*, 38:1–27.
———— (1969b), Fantasy, memory, and reality testing. *Psychoanal. Quart.*, 38:28–51.
———— (1980), Object concept and object choice. *Psychoanal. Quart.*, 49:109–133.
Breuer, J. & Freud, S. (1895), Studies on Hysteria. *Standard Edition*, 2. London: Hogarth Press, 1956.
Freud, S. (1920), Beyond the pleasure principle. *Standard Edition*, 18:7–64. London: Hogarth Press, 1955.
Nunberg, H. (1951), Transference and reality. *Internat. J. Psycho-Anal.*, 32:1–9.
Stolorow, R., Brandchaft, B., & Atwood, G. (1983), Intersubjectivity in psychoanalytic treatment with special reference to archaic states. *Bull. Menninger Clin.*, 47:117–128.

Valenstein, A.F. (1973), On attachment to painful feelings and the negative therapeutic reaction. *Psychoanalytic Study of the Child*, 28:365–392. New Haven: Yale University Press.

——— Reporter (1974), Panel on 'Transference.' *Internat. J. Psycho-Anal.*, 55:311–321.

——— (1979), The concept of "classical" psychoanalysis. *J. Amer. Psychoanal. Assn.*, 27 (Suppl.):113–136.

# 11

## Concluding Remarks

EVELYNE ALBRECHT SCHWABER, M.D.

In conclusion let us turn to the final question posed in the introduction to this volume: do the variety of viewpoints presented, despite their significant differences, retain nonetheless a fundamental commonality with the ideas expressed in Freud's postscript to the Dora case? In considering this question, let me briefly highlight some of these differences and the distinguishing emphases made by each of the contributors—recognizing that such summations may not do justice to the richness and scope of their views.

Michels notes that some of the dilemmas posed about the understanding of transference, can, if put to closer scrutiny, be seen to collapse. Transference is always past and present, intrapsychic and interpersonal, and much of the seeming tension is a matter of preferred definition. Michels takes the view that patients can be comprehended from multiple frames of reference, that theories vary in their applicability in different situations. Although essential, theories must not be taken as facts; they are myths and, as such, valuable creative products. He cautions against an "overinterest in theory" rather than in clinically derived data with which to make interpretations.

Valenstein espouses the view that interpretations and insight—in a verbal, explanatory sense—have their primary role in psychoanalysis where they elucidate oedipal transferences and the intrapsychic conflicts expressed within them. In psychotherapy, and particularly when working with patients with more primitive pathology, treatment is efficacious on a more experiential, enactive level. Preoedipal transferences are of a different order from oedipal transferences. Interpretations are not mutatively effective for preverbal phenomena in the same way as for later developmental issues, because they draw predominantly upon an "affect prescience" and not upon discretely laid down memories. Valenstein stresses the need for conservatism with regard to theoretical revision.

Ornstein argues for a novel conceptualization of the selfobject transference, a theoretical shift he feels will lend new meaning to the clinical material and allow for recognition of the patient's "thwarted need to grow." He stresses that one should look particularly for "transference disruptions" in elucidating this need. Ornstein maintains that preverbal phenomena reflected in the transference can be interpreted on the level of "verbally expressible insights" by their being "telescoped" into view at later developmental moments. His main emphasis is that the data suggest a fundamental revision of theory based on Kohut's model of the bipolar self.

Galenson contends that we look for reflections, even in oedipal transferences, of early, preoedipal features and for evidences of "the primordial relation to the mother" — although these may have to be arrived at more speculatively than the oedipal aspects. Noting that one's clinical acuity in recognizing these features is sharpened if one also works with very young children, she strongly advocates that therapists have this experience. Galenson also points out significant gender distinctions in preoedipal development, which will subsequently be manifest in different transference formations.

Gill emphasizes analysis of the transference as the central and defining feature of psychoanalysis, which, he believes, can be conducted in a "broader range of conditions" (e.g., with regard to setting, frequency of sessions, or severity of pathology) than is usually considered applicable. Gill defines psychotherapy by the absence of this primary position of the analysis of transference. He highlights an interactional view in which the therapeutic setting is an interpersonal one—that is, the experience "for both parties is to be understood as an interaction between them"; thereby, he stresses the more salient role of the present in relation to the past. He argues that he holds a fundamentally different perspective regarding the relativity of reality from that espoused by other contributors.

Arlow highlights the need to see the transference as a "derivative expression of an unconscious fantasy." He underscores three principles of mental functioning in understanding transference—dynamics, conflict, and compromise formation. As a compromise formation, the transference expresses a "persistent unconscious conflict over a wish from childhood." By virtue of the intrusion of the unconscious fantasy into conscious experience, the patient tries, in the transference, "to foist a role upon the therapist," resulting in a distortion of perception. Arlow asserts his agreement with the view of reality advanced by Gill—that the therapist does not know any final, absolute reality and has no claim to any "superior knowledge" as to the "real nature of the events" that transpire.

Thus, while some of the dilemmas posed in the introduction have become clarified or have receded, others have come more sharply to the fore:

1. *The nature of the therapeutic efficacy in the pre-oedipal transferences*: Are interpretations mutative in a verbal, explanatory sense, or is it primarily the affective experience that lends therapeutic impact?

2. *The nature of the relationship between theory and*

*technique*: Does theory help or hinder one's technical ability? How actively should theory be revised in accordance with shifting clinical findings or changes in technique?

3. *The extent to which the emergence of the transference is predetermined or, conversely, the degree to which it is affected (even in the initial hours) by the therapist's interventions*: How does one's view on this matter bear on the clinical emphasis placed on the role of the past relative to that of the present, and to the role of the intrapsychic in relation to the interpersonal? Is this a position influenced by one's outlook as to the essential unknowability of reality?

4. *The extent to which the transference, in psychoanalytic psychotherapy, should be directly and explicitly interpreted*: Is it even possible to recognize and articulate it other than in derivatives?

These are, then, some of the lingering tensions reflecting significant differences among the contributors. Let us now return to the Dora postscript and review the essential features of Freud's discovery:

1. The transference is inevitable and ubiquitous. It is not created by analysis, only brought to light there.

2. The transference revives the past in the present (the past experienced as though belonging to the person of the therapist). The parallel from past to present may be direct or there may be present-day revisions.

3. The transference, if recognized and interpreted, can be the most powerful ally to the treatment. It is essential that it be elucidated.

Strikingly, as we can see, these views bring the authors together. Freud's ideas, so powerfully articulated here, underlie the common thread basic to each of the presentations, remaining as cogent and relevant today as at the time of their discovery. (Freud was, of course, speaking of psychoanalysis. As indicated, there are differences among the contributors as to the efficacy and wisdom of transference interpretation in psychotherapy.)

Freud also highlights a further point. The transference, he writes, is elusive; it is very hard to tease out—"by far the hardest part of the whole task." Thus, he holds himself, not Dora's resistance here, responsible for his "neglect" in seeking out the "unknown quantity" within him—"the first signs of transference"—thereby bringing the analysis to a halt.

Why does he, in sharing this "failure," write as though it were a warning to us to heed that "unknown quantity" lest we, too, find that the transference takes us "unawares"? I believe there are some far-reaching implications in this note of caution.

Freud's monumental shift from the seduction to the fantasy theory of neurosogenesis marked a critical turning point in the history of psychoanalysis, placing psychic reality as its decisive clinical domain. What we can "know" of the external world is a product of our inner life—that is, of how we experience and perceive it. Reality (as discussed in Part II) cannot be absolutely knowable. Its assessment is a psychic function and must then contain within it the presence of the observer. This shift in Freud's view, as I have earlier indicated, can be seen as the reflection in depth psychology of the scientific revolution of our century, the era of relativity. J. A. Wheeler, the physicist, writes, "What we conceive of as reality is a few iron posts of observation with papier-maché construction between them that is but the elaborate work of our imagination" (1979).

The transference is the locus of psychic reality; by its recognition and elucidation we come to know another's inner world. The transference defines the view that what we see of another is a product of what we bring to it and, in turn, that what we experience within must contain what we perceive of the world outside. It is the attunement to both of these dimensions that has been, as Freud experienced it, so elusive.

Repeatedly in the history of psychoanalysis there have been challenges to the fantasy theory, with opponents strongly arguing that we must give greater regard to nurture, to the external events as such, in human development and experience. This view is correctly assessed as disputing the very core of psychoanalysis, for it is the specific focus on psychic reality that is being questioned. What is less readily recognized is that a similar challenge is posed by those who, while contending that ours is the purview of inner experience, fail to address—in any systematic way—the central position of the contribution of the "external" *as it is perceived*, that is, the salient role of perception as intrinsic to inner experience; thereby, a major component of the patient's *psychic reality* goes unattended.

The recognition that at all times, and even unknowingly, we participate in the patient's experience highlights Freud's admonition that we seek out the way in which we do so by directing our inquiry to it—to "some detail in our relations, or in [our] person or circumstances"—lest the transference take us unawares. It is this participation—because it may feel so different to us than to our patients—that can repeatedly escape our notice. Indeed, it is very difficult to maintain the position in our clinical attunement, even if we uphold it on theoretical grounds, that we cannot be the final arbiter of what has taken place and that all we can "know" is the meaning the patient attaches to it.[1]

Returning, then, to some of the recurring tensions, we may see their persistence as reflecting a lingering ambiguity on this elusive issue of psychic reality. The pull, for example, between inner and outer, "intrapsychic" and "interpersonal," may betray a continuing lack of clarity as to

[1]For further elaboration of these ideas see Schwaber, 1983, and in press.

whether by "interpersonal" one is referring to something of the "outside" that is "real" in an objective sense, to what the therapist *really* meant, or to what *really* happened in the patient's life—in the present or in the past—or solely to what is intrapsychically reflected.

Similarly, the issue of the relation between theory and technique, which seems so abidingly to defy resolution, may pose such a difficult problem because it does not of itself address the vantage point from which the therapist *listens* to the clinical material. Different theoretical models may change the options as to what and whether to interpret, but the overall clinical stance is influenced less by the choice of model than by the therapist's outlook on reality. Although there is some agreement with the general position that reality is essentially unknowable,[2] and that inner experience is therefore our domain of investigation, the specific ways in which this view is translated into how one listens in relation to the transference may warrant further articulation.

Wheeler (1979, 1981) has stated, "We are not only observers. We are participators . . . inescapably involved in bringing about that which appears to be happening. . . . For our picture of the world this is the most revolutionary thing discovered. We still have not come to terms with it." This is what Freud so brilliantly discovered in the field of depth psychology; the transference is "the hardest part of the whole task. . . . the one thing the presence of which has to be detected . . . with only the slightest clues to go upon." The full clinical implications of this embarkment into the scientific era of relativity may be still early in the process of realization, and indeed may be the undercurrent of much that is being debated.

[2]See for example chapters 9 and 10.

# References

Schwaber, E. (1983), Psychoanalytic listening and psychic reality. *Internat. Rev. Psycho-Anal.*, 10:379–392.

———— (in press), Reconstruction and perceptual experience: Some further thoughts on psychoanalytic listening. *J. Amer. Psychoanal.* Assn.

Wheeler, J.A. (1979), Quoted in: Probing the universe, by S. Begley.*Newsweek* (March 12).

———— (1981). This participatory universe. Unpublished manuscript.

# Name Index

177

# Subject Index